YORK MEDIEVAL TEXTS

General Editors

ELIZABETH SALTER & DEREK PEARSALL

Middle English Romances

A. C. GIBBS

Northwestern University Press
Evanston
1966

First published in the U.S.A. 1966 by
Northwestern University Press
under arrangement with Edward Arnold (Publishers) Ltd., London

Library of Congress Catalog Card Number: 66-27661

Preface

The present series of *York Medieval Texts* is designed for undergraduates and, where the text is appropriate, for upper forms of schools. Its aim is to provide editions of major pieces of Middle English writing in a form which will make them accessible without loss of historical authenticity. Texts are chosen because of their importance and artistic merit, and individual volumes may contain a single work, coherent extracts from a longer work, or representative examples of a genre. The principle governing the presentation of the text is to preserve the character of the English while eliminating unnecessary encumbrances such as obsolete letters and manuscript errors. Glossary and explanatory notes operate together to clarify the text; special attention is paid to the interpretation of passages which are syntactically rather than lexically difficult. The Introduction to each volume, like the rest of the apparatus, is designed to set the work in its proper literary context, and to provide the critical guidance most helpful to present-day readers. The intention of the series is exclusively literary: the Editors hope to attract a wider audience not only for works within the accepted literary canon, but also for those which have until now been regarded as 'specialist' in appeal, or which have been presented as if they were.

This volume of extracts from *Medieval Romances* focusses critical attention upon a significant but unwieldy body of Middle English writings by offering examples of them at their moments of truth. The excerpts are chosen in accordance with a governing critical concept elaborated in the editor's Introduction; they thus enable the reader to relate form to function, representative to type, in a coherent and meaningful manner. The Introduction takes full account of what has been best and most recently said by scholars on the subject of 'Romance', but is alive to the needs of the modern reader, assuming that the search for understanding and historical orientation does not obscure, but rather enhances enjoyment of the poetry.

Acknowledgements

I am indebted to the authorities of the following bodies for permission to print from MSS under their care, and for supplying me with photographic reproductions of them: The British Museum, the Bodleian Library, the Cambridge University Library, the National Library of Scotland, the Glasgow University Library. I also owe a great debt to the General Editors of the *York Medieval Series*, Elizabeth Salter and Derek Pearsall, for the helpful care with which they have read my drafts.

I should like further to thank the University of York for a grant towards my expenses in preparing this book.

Contents

Introduction

' "Bitzer," said Thomas Gradgrind. "Your definition of a horse."

"Quadruped. Graminivorous. Forty teeth, namely, twenty-four grinders, four eye-teeth, and twelve incisive. Sheds coat in the spring; in marshy country sheds hoofs too. Hoofs hard, but requiring to be shod with iron. Age known by marks in mouth." Thus (and much more) Bitzer.

"Now, girl number twenty," said Mr Gradgrind. "You know what a horse is." '

(Charles Dickens, Hard Times)

Since this introduction is largely concerned with definitions, the above quotation from *Hard Times* is meant to serve as a reminder of the dangers of too great a reliance upon them. 'Girl number twenty' is, of course, Sissy Jupe, who, having grown up in Sleary's Horseriding, has known horses all her life without being able to 'define' them. Similarly, when we talk in general terms about a phenomenon called 'The Medieval Romance' we are only too likely to find that its essential nature escapes from all our formulations. We may well find that the mode of instruction favoured by Mr Wackford Squeers is of more use to us than Mr Gradgrind's, for at Dotheboys Hall, an understanding of the concept 'horse' involved grooming Squeers's own animal. For that reason, I have selected a number of poems and extracts from poems commonly classified as medieval romances, with the intention of presenting them, not as an anthology, but as extended quotations illustrating an argument about the nature of romance.

It may be helpful to start by examining a few of the contemporary usages of 'Romance' and 'Romantic', to clarify our expectations of the terms, before we go on to see whether they shed any light on the medieval works we have to consider. Perhaps the most influential of modern definitions is that of 'Romanticism' as a theory of art. This is the Oxford English Dictionary's definition:

'the movement in literature (and art) originating in a revolt against the formalities and conventions of classicism, and characterized in the nineteenth century by conscious preoccupation with the subjective and imaginative aspects of nature and life.'

Some remarks from D. W. Harding's chapter on 'The Character of Literature' in Volume V of *The Pelican Guide to English Literature (From Blake to Byron)* may serve as a further gloss. Romanticism exemplifies:

'the individual testing of standards in all directions . . . '

'the use of fantasy as a means of expressing emotional experience not

A*

sanctioned by conventional good sense and not strictly accountable to reason.'

'Their (the Romantics') exact intention could not be formulated in advance; it reached definition only in what the language actually produced when they worked in it, rather as a sculptor's exact intention cannot exist apart from the materials that define it. This attitude harmonized well with the romantic conception of the poet as seer.' (pp. 36-7, 63)

Such attitudes have nothing in common with formulated medieval aesthetic theory:[1] on the other hand, such theory had little or nothing to say about a secular and vernacular form such as the romance. It is, then, open to us in the course of this discussion to determine whether such definitions of Romanticism in art as those proffered above release to us any of the potential of the medieval art-form which we call Romance.

Apart from that, 'Romance' is a common enough word in all our vocabularies. We use it most commonly, perhaps, in talking about a human sexual relationship. This relationship is not one of physical gratification alone, nor is it a conventional marriage entered into for reasons primarily social or even economic. The word denotes a particular sentimental attitude to the relationship on both sides, and implies an adherence to codes of human behaviour which are neither purely physical, nor purely economic. In this we are, at many removes, the heirs of the Middle Ages.

'Romance' and 'Romantic' have also strong overtones of the exotic and outlandish. Tahiti, for example, is 'romantic' for us in a way that Wigan isn't, though it might be the other way about for a Tahitian. When we call a place or a setting 'romantic' we are recognizing its difference from our normal humdrum surroundings. In it, we may be able to escape from the everyday pressures of existence and cultivate a more ideal mode of behaviour–and this notion, too, has some significance in our enquiry. And thirdly, a less common usage still has relevance. Someone who 'romances' is a liar, a dealer in extravagant fictions: for our purpose the association of the Romance with fiction, in distinction from other forms of narrative, is of very long standing.

It is when we turn to the specialized meaning given to 'Romance' by the literary historians that our troubles start. It is not so difficult to say what is *meant* by the term in literary histories or bibliographies, for it is generally used as a hold-all in which to stow whatever verse or prose narratives cannot be more neatly packaged as epic, chronicle, hagiography or fabliau: it is rather more difficult to convince ourselves that we can usefully talk *as critics* about such a random and heterogeneous collection of works in terms of a distinct *genre*. In fact, in medieval literary history, 'Romance' is used in two senses: generally,

[1] For recent discussions of this see D. W. Robertson, *A Preface to Chaucer* (Princeton, 1963), and C. S. Lewis, *The Discarded Image* (Cambridge, 1964)

of fictional narrative, concerning, in the main, aristocratic personages, and more specifically in the sense given first place by the Oxford English Dictionary:

> 'A tale in verse, embodying the life and adventures of some hero of chivalry and belonging in matter and form to the age of knighthood; also in later use a prose tale of a similar character.'

The task, as I see it, is for the critic to determine how far the works contained in the bibliographers' hold-all embody the ideals of chivalry and belong to the age of knighthood.

What we should notice first here is that this definition is historically anchored (to the 'age of knighthood') just as the Dictionary's definition of Romanticism was quite firmly anchored to the nineteenth century. It is vital to bear this in mind, because there are large numbers of works current in the Middle Ages which we might well agree to call 'Romances' on a variety of counts but which do *not* 'belong' in any essential way to 'the age of knighthood'. Further, the above definition uses the concept of the hero—not simply as the leading figure in a work of fiction, but as a special kind of man. Here it becomes necessary, in order to define Romance, to say a few words about the Epic, for the concept of the hero is something which unites them, something which makes it possible to call the chivalric romance an epic of the feudal age, as Auerbach does.[2] The epic poem celebrates the achievements of some heroic personage of history or tradition, and a useful discussion of the classical Greek concept of the hero can be found in Sir Maurice Bowra's *Heroic Poetry:*

> ' . . . the early Greek philosophers gave a special place to those men who live for action and for the honour which comes from it. Such, they believed, are moved by an important element in the human soul, the self-assertive principle, which is to be distinguished equally from the appetite and from the reason and realizes itself in great deeds. They held . . . that the man who seeks honour is himself an honourable figure. . . . In the ordeals of the heroic life his full worth is tested and revealed. It is not even necessary that he should be rewarded by success: the hero who dies in battle after doing his utmost is in some ways more admirable than he who lives. In either case he is honoured because he has made a final effort in courage and endurance, and no more can be asked of him. He gives dignity to the human race by showing what feats it is capable of; he extends the bounds of experience for others and enhances their appreciation of life by the example of his abundant vitality.'[3]

[2] E. Auerbach, *Mimesis*, tr. Willard Trask (Doubleday Anchor Books, New York, 1957), p. 111. My principal debt in this introduction is to this book, in particular chapters 5 and 6

[3] Sir Maurice Bowra, *Heroic Poetry* (London, 1952), pp. 1, 4

The way in which this is conveyed in heroic epic poetry is by an objective presentation of what the heroes are and do: it depends on a shared ideal of manhood and honour, and on a view of existence in which man plays a central part. Heroic poetry proper is anthropocentric, Bowra argues: though Homer introduces gods into his action, man is always the true focus of attention. The Homeric gods are less noble than men because they have nothing to define and limit their activity. Men are bound by claims and obligations of many kinds and in their devotion to these, to the ideal of manhood which embodies them, and in their mortality, their nobility lies. To illustrate this point, not from epic but from romance, we might say that it is meaningless to compare the Green Knight's courage in facing the beheading test with Gawain's, once it has become apparent that the Green Knight has supernatural resources and cannot be killed. It is the definition of human potential by the fact of mortality that makes Gawain's courage meaningful.

In the terms that Bowra suggests, then, it is certainly possible to talk of Romance as a variant form of Epic. This is a point which needs stressing, for influential books like Ker's *Epic and Romance*[4] and Southern's *The Making of the Middle Ages*[5] have tended to stress the differences between the two forms to a point where their similarities are perhaps obscured. A helpful indication of the relationship between the two is given by consideration of the Homeric epics. The *Odyssey* as opposed to the *Iliad* has strong Romance qualities, in that the story concentrates on the wanderings of a single hero (though *Odysseus* has his crew with him) through a world of strangeness and fantasy. There are three ideas here: first, that of the search or quest, which Auerbach singles out as the dominant narrative device of the medieval chivalric romance; second, the hero is acting, comparatively speaking, as an individual hero rather than as the representative of his society; third, the action takes place largely in an exotic setting which is exploited as distinct from the everyday world. All these ideas act as criteria whose value will be tested on the Middle English poems selected.

There are, besides, other classical and post-classical works which most authorities agree to call Romances on rather different grounds—grounds which we can best understand if we examine those plays of Shakespeare which are usually put into this category: *Pericles, The Winter's Tale, The Tempest*. The characteristic plot-elements in these plays—the separation and disruption of families, followed by an eventual reunion and reconciliation, the love of a virtuous young hero and heroine, the recovery of lost royal children—all these features correspond to, and in many cases derive from, the plots of the

[4] W. P. Ker, *Epic and Romance* (Dover Books, New York, 1957)

[5] R. W. Southern, *The Making of the Middle Ages* (Grey Arrow Books, London, 1959)

Greek romances of the post-classical period. Again, the issues are private rather than public, and the fates of nations need not be directly involved. The plots are governed by chance: there is no great desire for a rational chain of cause and effect, and the writers are concerned to exploit surprise and curiosity in their audience. They have love as their central theme—primarily the sentimental passion of a young man and woman, but also married, filial or parental love. All these features occur frequently in those medieval works classified as romances (including several illustrated in this book) without really indicating the specific quality of the *medieval* type.

If we now narrow the field of inquiry to Western Europe in the Dark Ages and the early medieval period proper, we find that the characteristic form of narrative poetry is the national heroic epic—poems like the German *Hildebrandslied*, the Scandinavian *Helgakvitha* or the English *Beowulf*, which, in the last analysis, relate to actual historical and political situations, and whose heroes act in some way as representatives of their people, even though their conscious motivation is heroic self-assertion. The most significant development of this type is the Old French *chanson de geste*, for in it we find the adaptation of the ideal of the heroic life to the concepts of feudalism and of Christianity, the two most distinctive medieval influences on this mode of literature. The greatest of the *chansons de geste*, *La Chanson de Roland*, represents a feudal situation. Charlemagne is in effect a Prince of God, the head of Christendom and the paragon of knighthood, while the hero Roland fights as a vassal of the Emperor and of God—his relationship to both being expressed in exactly comparable terms—even though he is actually seen to be motivated by a highly personal desire for glory. Now as Southern points out:

'Nobility had only two roots during this period: property, by which a man entered into a set of relationships determining his place in society; and knighthood, by which he assumed responsibilities and privileges denied to those outside the ranks of the fraternity. The property relationship was born in the act of homage; the knightly relationship in the act of initiation to knighthood. The first gave a man a place in a hierarchy; the second in a brotherhood. The man who had many lords by his homage was on an equality with the king by his knighthood. It is not surprising therefore that the first was the practical working bond between men, while the second had almost from the first something of romance and idealism and ineffectiveness.' (p. 116)

In this distinction we find perhaps the essential difference between Epic and Romance in the feudal age. In the *chanson de geste* a knight setting out on a journey has an office and a place in a politico-historical context, in a social hierarchy. The characters who take part in the action have a function in the real world—the defence of Charlemagne's kingdom against the infidels, their conquest and conversion, for example. Such are the political and historical purposes served by the feudal ethos which the knights profess. But in the chivalric romance this ethos serves no practical reality at all: it has become absolute and its only purpose is self-realization. What are the first signs of this change in the literature?

If we turn now to the origins of the word 'Romance', we find that it originally denoted anything pertaining to Rome: in particular, those languages like French which derived from popular Latin. The first use of the word which has literary significance is that applying to works of translation from Latin into the vernacular, and among the earliest examples is a group of three adaptations of classical or pseudo-classical epics, made in France in the mid-twelfth century: the *Roman de Thebes* (c 1150) from Statius's *Thebaid*, the *Eneas* (1155) from Virgil, and Benoit de Saint-Maure's *Roman de Troie* (c 1160), based on two Latin prose accounts of the Trojan War which claim the authority respectively of two eye-witnesses, Dares Phrygius and Dictys Cretensis. The origin of these works is in classical epic: what critical significance, then, can attach to their title of *Roman?* There is a long-standing argument that indigenous epic becomes romance when transplanted, and Muscatine restates it when he argues for the significance of these works being imitations of *classic* epic rather than of the contemporary epic form of the *chanson de geste*.[6] By this choice, their subject-matter was already more remote, learned and wonderful than that of native epic. Though a subject like the Trojan War was still seen as history, it was possible to take rather more liberties with its heroic values than perhaps it was with those values illustrated in Roland's fight against the Saracens at Roncesvalles. Thus, Benoit de Saint-Maure introduces three substantial love-stories into his lengthy account of the alarms and excursions of the siege, most notably the story of Troilus and Cressida, which is his invention. Love, though it was a dominant factor in the prose romances of Greece, played a smaller part—if it was present at all—in the national epics of France and England.[7] Alde, the sister of Oliver, and Roland's betrothed, merely hovers disconsolately in the wings until, at the news of Roland's death, she is allowed her one significant gesture—which is to die for love. The heroines of medieval romance, however, are much nearer the centre of the stage, even if they do not actually dominate the poems in which they appear. In the introduction of a strong love-element, then, these pseudo-classical French poems can be called precursors of the true chivalric romance: the love-affair between Aeneas and Lavinia is the real centre of interest of the twelfth-century

[6] C. Muscatine, *Chaucer and the French Tradition* (Berkeley, 1960), p. 12
[7] The women in German and Norse epic are more prominent, but they are heroic in their own right.

adaptation of Virgil's epic. Nevertheless, we should remember that it is not simply the introduction of a love-interest into the plot that will make a narrative into a romance, under any critically useful definition of the term, but the distinctive way in which the love-relationship is treated.

These poems were called *romans* because they were vernacular renderings of Latin works, yet we can, in fact, see that they have features in common which come ultimately to be characteristic of a literary form called 'Medieval Romance'. These features are: the choice of exotic subject-matter, instead of imitation of the native epic mode; an unprecedented space and importance given to love-episodes; the taste for marvellous descriptions and elaborate settings; a courtly social aura; and a new verse-form, the octosyllabic couplet as opposed to the monorhymed *laisses* of the *chansons de geste*. They are, of course, not the only twelfth-century French poems to be called *romans*, and we can see the need for caution with the term when we consider that Wace's two long verse-chronicles, *Le Roman de Brut* and *Le Roman de Rou*, share the appellation. These are comparatively sober and factual accounts of historical events, or events believed to be historical. Nevertheless, Wace has something in common with the other poems. He shares the verse-form and the social aura, and when love-situations arise, they are developed, however slightly, along similar lines. On the evidence so far presented, then, we can talk of medieval romance as a style, a manner of treating certain literary situations. We are now to see how it becomes a self-governing form, a coherent attitude to experience.

The essential factor here is the notion of chivalry—more essential, in my view, to *medieval* romance than the love-theme, for the latter is usually, though not always, represented as an inevitable part of the chivalric ethos. Chivalry is not, of course, exclusive to romance: the *chansons de geste* also study and depict a knightly class. But the chivalric romance has, as Auerbach says, for its fundamental purpose, 'a self-portrayal of feudal knighthood with its mores and ideals' (p. 114). The feudal hierarchy of Charlemagne's empire gradually gives way to Arthur's Round Table, the brotherhood of knights sustained, not by material or political considerations but by common adherence to an ideal of knighthood. No single definition will suffice for this ideal, for every original poet who treats of chivalry will give his own emphasis to the concepts which make it up. As Southern points out:

> 'Fundamentally, knighthood was the rite of entry into the ranks of the mounted warrior. But . . . as time went on, knighthood responded to every wind that blew; without ever becoming religious it enjoyed the sanction and colour of a religious setting; it obtained a place in the philosophy of political and social life; it inspired a great literature and was swept into a romantic movement wholly alien to its origins.' (p. 117)

Nevertheless, the following qualities can reasonably be considered constants:

courage, loyalty, mutual respect, refined manners, service to women. The first two or three would apply equally as well to the epic hero as to the hero of romance. The difference is that in romance they exist as absolutes, not in significant relationship to any real political situation. This becomes plain when we look at the occasions in romance when such qualities are displayed. The knights reveal them, not in 'their lordes war', not in any realistically motivated political or religious cause, but in *aventure*, knightly adventure. The great theme of the chivalric romance is self-realization—in the best work, the adventures are not there for their own sake, but to call forth the very essence of the knight's ideal of manhood. To quote from one of the most famous of medieval romances, *Huon of Bordeaux*:

' . . . I toke on me that any adventure that I myght here of, though it were never so perelous that I shulde never eschew it for any fere of deth.'

' . . . I departyd out of Fraunce for none other thynge but to serche the straunge adventures.'[8]

The replacement of the military expedition by the solitary adventure, of warfare by the feat of arms—these two features of the chivalric romance are intimately linked with two other important features: the use of an exotic, magic or otherworldly setting, and the use of love as the commonest plot-motivation. To take the setting first: we have seen that our contemporary expectations of 'Romance' include an exotic location, a kind of idealism of description and the creation of a sensuous atmosphere. The earliest works which we agree to call romantic have these qualities—the *Odyssey* is a tale of wonder, so are the Greek romances, so, to a high degree, are the late plays of Shakespeare. But are the medieval romances like this? It is remarkable on how few occasions we can honestly answer 'Yes'. One of the poems in this selection, *Sir Orfeo*, has the kind of 'romantic' atmosphere we might expect, and most readers would agree that *Sir Gawain and the Green Knight* successfully exploits a sense of mystery. But these are exceptions; all too often we find the most fantastic marvels presented in the most flat and matter-of-fact manner. We have to determine whether this indicates the authors' incompetence, or our own misguided reading.

Our sense of what is romantic in a setting or a description depends on what we are used to, on the contrast between normality and what is described. It is possible that a perfectly flat and matter-of-fact account of 'foreign parts'—perhaps the description of the Sultan's palace in any of the romances using Oriental story-matter—might have seemed more wonderful, more 'romantic' to a medieval audience than what might seem to us a far more 'atmospheric'

[8] From Lord Berners' English prose version, *Huon of Burdeux*, ed. S. L. Lee, E.E.T.S., E.S. 40-1 (1882-3), ch. xxxii, pp. 97, 98

account of magical occurrences set in France or England. If poet and audience share a belief in the supernatural, there is no great need for an effort of persuasion on the poet's part. Here, then, may be one reason why we rarely find romantic atmosphere in the medieval romance. Another influential factor, however, may be that the bulk of surviving *English* romances are the work of inferior poets. Though the medieval romance as a form does not appear to depend upon atmosphere, yet the best poets provide it, and in such a way as to further their central purpose.[9]

Let us now consider the function of the exotic setting. We think of romance as an escapist form of literature, and in an important way it is so. As Arnold Kettle (whom, as he is a Marxist, one would not expect to be sympathetic towards the form) points out:

> 'Romance in the first place delights and entertains the rulers without bringing them face to face with realities they would sooner put behind them. . . . In the second place it builds, for the edification and pleasure of those unfortunate enough to find themselves outside the priviliged *élite*, a fantasy, a pseudo-world, seductive or sad, delightful or horrible, which has one unfailing quality: that, however remote it may be from reality, the values and attitudes it incorporates are such as are least likely to undermine the theories and practice of class society.'[10]

But he goes on to say that it is not enough to label this world escapist and imagine one has explained it away, nor is it enough to refer to romance's idealized picture of the world 'as though idealization were a form of original sin and needed no more explicit condemnation' (p. 35). Romance is certainly an idealization: the chivalric romance disengages the knightly class from worldly concerns, quite deliberately. This idealization affects the mode of presentation: the romance, in giving its picture of how life is lived, deals in superlatives:

> 'With alle the wele of the worlde thay woned ther samen,
> The most kyd knyghtez under Krystes selven,
> And the lovelokkest ladies that ever lif haden,
> And he the comlokest kyng that the court haldes.'[11]

[9] For an excellent discussion of the treatment of the supernatural in the romances see the chapter, 'A Characterization of the English Medieval Romances' in D. Everett, *Essays on Middle English Literature* (Oxford, 1955)

[10] Arnold Kettle, *An Introduction to the English Novel* (Grey Arrow Books, 1962), Vol. I, p. 34

[11] *Sir Gawain and the Green Knight*, edd. J. R. R. Tolkien, E. V. Gordon (Oxford, 1925), lines 50–3

Thus, the poor, the deformed, the uncouth have nothing to do with chivalry: they can have no function in the courtly romance except as guides, minor enemies or objects of charity. The ideal is not subjected to the gross impact of events; accordingly much of the description in this tradition is static and formal. Frequently, it does not serve the dramatic action of the poem, but points toward its ultimate significance. Muscatine, indeed, suggests:

> 'The idealism of romance is in some ways a transposed Christian idealism. . . . The medieval audience is ready and able to see effortlessly beyond the surface representation of form and image to a higher reality, to see the concrete itself as metaphor and symbol.' (p. 14)

This helps to explain the exoticism of the setting: it may be ancient Greece, Rome or Carthage, as in those twelfth-century French poems; or the Britain of King Arthur, a Britain which has lost its historical personality; or a dreamland quite outside geography. Such locations, unlike Charlemagne's empire, supply an excellent setting for adventure in the nearly abstract:

> 'Freed from the exigencies of time and place, the hero can concentrate on his courtly quest. To cross over on a sword-bridge into a land whence no stranger has ever returned—for the love of a Lady—is an act of gratuitous valour that no-one can quibble about.' (p. 15)

Yet, on the whole, the writers of medieval chivalric romance did not invent this dreamland. Sometimes they borrowed their settings from classical models, or from the lost 'golden age' of their own lands. Sometimes they took over the travellers' tales of those who had visited remote places—the Orient in particular furnished them with an ideal setting, and it seems clear that extensive use was made of information gathered from returning crusaders. But the most distinctive source of material, for plot as well as setting, was the vast body of Celtic folk-tale. How this came about is by no means clear, but the Normans were in close contact with Celtic peoples both in Brittany and Wales, and obviously the material is inherently attractive as narrative. It must be insisted, however, that much of it seems to have been taken over for the specific purpose of providing *aventures* which would illustrate the ideal values of chivalry. The difficulty is, however, that the material had an essential *sen* or meaning of its own[12] which was, in many cases, a form of one of the archetypal human myths. Thus, behind *Sir Gawain and the Green Knight* lies, unmistakably, a vegetation myth, an attempt to explain the processes of growth and decay in the cycle of the seasons in anthropomorphic terms. And Lancelot's crossing

---

[12] The useful terms *sen* and *matière* have been borrowed by the critics from the great French romance-writer, Chrétien de Troyes. In the introduction to his *Lancelot* he says that the material (*matière*) and the treatment (*sen*) are given and furnished to him by the Countess of Champagne, his patron

the sword-bridge into the Land of Gorre seems no less clearly an episode from a mythical exploration of the subject of death and the possibility of an afterlife. If the romance writers had known this (and there is no real evidence that they did) they would have said, I think, that though this might be the *sen* of the *matière* (the story-matter) they had adopted, they were quite within their rights in disregarding it and imposing their own *sen*—the chivalric significance —in its stead. So the Beheading Game is not, in my view, a ritual undertaken to unfreeze the life-processes and bring back the Spring, but a means of testing the chivalric virtue of the hero. Similarly, Lancelot's exploit does not testify to man's conquest over death, but to the power of Lancelot's devotion to Guinevere. It may still happen, however, that in spite of the poet's conscious shaping of his material, the old archetypal power of the myth may persist and exert its influence over us, transferred from the poet's subconscious to ours. It is a matter of the individual's response to the poem: if it is to happen, it will happen, but let us not seek it at the cost of disregarding the author's clear intention.[13]

Lancelot crosses the sword-bridge as a testimony of his devotion to Guinevere, and this brings us to the final topic of this general discussion: the function and treatment of love in the chivalric romance. Heterosexual love plays no important part in the epic as a whole: the epic hero loves glory, and the only emotional human relationship celebrated is that of the hero with his lord or his battle-companion. Sentimental love, however, is a fairly constant feature of most of the types of romance mentioned, and it is typical of the medieval chivalric romance also. Typical, indeed, but not of the essence: what is essential is the proving, the trial by adventure of the idealism of the knightly hero. But the romance poets, on the whole, were not prepared to present this process in an abstract and unmotivated fashion. In order to give an idealized picture of chivalry they had already divested their subject-matter of practical motivation through a political or historical context, and it is natural enough that Love should very frequently be adopted as a substitute for other possible motives. Further, love came generally, though not universally, to be regarded as an essential and obligatory ingredient of knightly perfection—as Southern reminds us, 'knighthood responded to every wind that blew'—and a certain attitude to love proved very congenial to the literary upholders of the chivalric ideal. It is most important to recognize that it is 'a certain attitude to love' and not love itself: there are many poems written in the medieval period which have a sentimental love-relationship between a man and a woman at the centre of

[13] The best statement of the anthropological approach is found in J. Speirs, *Medieval English Poetry* (London, 1957). His position is attacked by C. S. Lewis in 'The Anthropological Approach' in *English and Medieval Studies presented to J. R. R. Tolkien*, edd. N. Davis, C. L. Wrenn (London, 1962)

their action which are yet not the type of medieval romance (*Floriz and Blauncheflur*, of the poems selected, for example).

This special attitude to love is what is generally known as Courtly Love, although *fine amour*, 'refined love', is a more descriptive phrase for it. It is a highly controversial subject, one which even now is far from being fully explained. Discussion of it for the last thirty years has been dominated by C. S. Lewis's *The Allegory of Love*, and though recent criticism has clearly shown the limitations and over-simplifications of Lewis's thesis,[14] it is outlined here as still the most available. Some necessary *caveats* will appear in the course of the discussion. He lists the four marks of Courtly Love thus: Humility, Courtesy, Adultery, and the Religion of Love (p. 12). The lover is always in the position of the suppliant: the lady is traditionally desirable and difficult and her favours are not lightly given. The lover must prove himself worthy of love by humility and devoted service: even then he can never say with justice that he has deserved the lady's love. If she grants him her favour, it is because of her generosity, her *grace*, not because of his desert. Further, this love is highly likely to be adulterous (Lewis goes too far in making this a condition) even although it may have no physical manifestation at all, and it is seen in terms of a religion of love presided over by the God Amor.

Probably the hardest questions to answer are those which ask whether the code of *fine amour* had any existence outside literature, and whether, if it was really practised, this was because of its literary expression or vice versa. Actual social conditions go some way towards providing an explanation. It is obvious that in some of its aspects the image of the relationship between lover and mistress is strongly influenced by feudalism. The lover is the lady's vassal, and is bound to do her service, while her rights over him are more or less absolute. In the Christian feudal epic, Christianity appears in a feudal guise: thus, Roland is God's vassal as well as Charlemagne's, and when he dies, he offers his glove to God in the exact gesture of feudal homage to a temporal lord. The image is thus available for the writers of romance, and whether any actual human relationship in the period corresponded to the idealization of the courtly love romances is really a secondary question. Lewis's picture of the castle in Provence, dominated by the lady and her damsels, 'a little island of comparative leisure and luxury . . . in a barbarous countryside' (p. 12), in which the male population, in the lord's frequent absences, were feudally inferior to the lady, and were

---

[14] C. S. Lewis, *The Allegory of Love* (Oxford, 1936). Important contributions to the discussion, with criticisms of Lewis's position, will be found in D. S. Brewer's edition of *The Parlement of Foulys* (Nelson's Medieval and Renaissance Library, London, 1960), pp. 7–13; J. Lawlor, 'The Pattern of Consolation in *The Book of the Duchess*', *Chaucer Criticism*, edd. Richard J. Schoeck, Jerome Taylor (Notre Dame, Indiana, 1961), ii. 234–8

her 'men', has still some power to persuade. But the picture is highly fanciful, and, since the evidence for such a state of affairs is too often only literary, his argument frequently proceeds in a circle. It is clear enough, on the other hand, that much of the literary patronage of the twelfth century was in feminine hands. Whether or not a woman like Eleanor of Aquitaine, grand-daughter of William IX (one of the first of the troubadors) and queen successively of France and England, conducted her own love-affairs in the manner of the courtly romances, whether or not she actually held 'courts of love' in which nice points of *fine amour* were debated, she and others like her certainly encouraged the writing of poetry of this kind. The spread of lay literacy, with people reading privately, and writing for a private audience, generated of itself the kind of self-consciousness and mannered elaboration out of which the courtly code grew.

It is in arguments for this love being necessarily adulterous that Lewis perhaps oversimplifies most dangerously, yet even here there is much that is true in what he says, and any argument that puts *The Franklin's Tale*, which treats of *fine amour* in the context of marriage, nearer the centre of an account of medieval romance than Chrétien's *Lancelot* will be far more erroneous than Lewis's. He asserts:

> 'Marriages had nothing to do with love, and no "nonsense" about marriage was tolerated. All matches were matches of interest, and, worse still, of an interest that was continually changing. When the alliance which had answered was answering no longer, the husband's object was to get rid of the lady as soon as possible. Marriages were frequently dissolved. The same woman who was the lady and the "dearest dread" of her vassals was often little better than a piece of property to her husband.' (p. 13)

Once again we see an over-reliance on circular reasoning, a readiness to accept as social realism what we find in the romances: nevertheless the shaping influence of feudalism reveals itself again. Further, the Christian attitude to marriage in the Middle Ages also devalues the woman's status and tends to divest the marriage relationship of much of its emotional content. The social conditions seem to have been highly conducive to making 'the idealization of love the idealization of adultery'.

The other notable element of Courtly Love is its religiosity. To be brief, what happens to secular sentiment in this change, if we can still call it so, from epic to romance, happens also to religious sentiment.[15] The change from public to private fulfilment is seen in the new views of the function of monasticism, just as in the release of the knightly hero from a social role. The setting-up of the lady on a pedestal in the courtly convention parallels the developing

[15] See Southern, *op. cit.*, ch. 5

cult of the Virgin in religious literature: indeed Lewis argues (pp. 18–22) that
it parodies the cult, or deliberately sets itself up in opposition to it. The two
phenomena are, at the least, products of the same social situation.

Let us now look at these criteria in the light of an actual example, for it is
necessary at this stage of the argument to remind ourselves that perfect examples of the medieval chivalric romance, poems which illustrate all the features
which have been listed as in some sense typical, are very rare indeed. In the
Erec et Enide of Chrétien de Troyes, love is discussed within the terms of the
marriage relationship, and furthermore, the marriage looks very much like
a social contract between the hero and the heroine's father. Enide is quite
passive until after the marriage has taken place. Yet I would still maintain that
Erec is a chivalric romance, and is so in a much deeper sense than any of the
poems selected for discussion in this book. The important thing about love in
this poem isn't that it is married love rather than adultery, but that it is *educative*,
and that it supplies the motive for knightly adventure. Through Enide's love
for the hero, and ultimately through his love for her, he is brought to a full
realization of the meaning of his existence as a knight. This is the necessary
outcome of the ideal chivalric romance: the essential question to be asked
about any such poem is whether or not it is achieved.

We may now close this section with a re-assessment of the criteria accumula-
ted during the course of the argument. What relevance, first of all, have the
arguments from nineteenth-century Romanticism? Harding's phrase, 'the
individual testing of standards' might very tentatively be set beside the romance's concentration on the hero as an individual, as opposed to the representative national hero of epic, while the use of fantasy as a means of expressing
emotional experience is clearly a vital feature of the romance of any period.
Of the contemporary usages of 'romance' and 'romantic' also, most have some
point in our discussion, if we recognize the danger of too great an expectation
of 'atmospheric writing' in the medieval poems. We have also seen that a
general category called *romance* which included the Odyssey, the Greek prose
tales and Shakespeare's last plays as well as these poems would have some
validity, while recognizing that the distinctive qualities of *medieval* romance
can best be revealed by a study of feudalism.

The Medieval Romance in England

The earliest extant English romances, *King Horn* and *Floriz and Blauncheflur*,
are both to be found in a Cambridge University MS, Gg.4.27, which the most
recent palaeographical evidence dates at about 1240. The date is significant,
for it means that they are eighty or ninety years later than the earliest French
romances, the *Eneas*, the *Roman de Thebes* and the *Roman de Troie*. The medieval
chivalric romance was invented and brought to fulfilment in France by poets

like Chrétien de Troyes, who was writing between 1160 and the 1180s, and Guillaume de Lorris, whose *Roman de la Rose* was left incomplete at his death in 1237. As Muscatine says:

'By the time of Guillaume de Lorris, its (romance's) major potentialities as romance had all been fulfilled, and there were already beginning to appear, alongside a comparatively undisturbed main tradition, mutations and hybrids leading in a variety of directions: toward popular debasement, toward mystical, religious sublimation, and toward comic and ironic reconstruction. (p. 12)

There are very few 'mainstream' romances in English. Even *Sir Gawain and the Green Knight* and the romances of Chaucer go beyond the sanctions of the original form, while in general the history of romance in England (with a few exceptions) is one of popular debasement. However, the facts that even the earliest English romances are written in what might be called the decadence of the form, and that the finest English examples are produced in the fourteenth and even the fifteenth centuries, when the best poets in Europe are going on to other things, should not be considered on their own. It is possible, here as everywhere else in medieval literature, that much early work has been lost. There is some evidence to suggest this, but the leading authority on 'lost literature', R. M. Wilson, is cautious in his estimate of what has been lost:

'On the whole, it is unlikely that many romances of the three great Matters (*i.e.* Rome, France and Britain) have been lost. So far as we can tell, these romances, at any rate in England, appear to have been a distinctively literary development, so that they were assured of a written existence.'[16]

Wilson thinks, however, that we may have lost some romances on specifically *English* subjects: *King Horn* and *Havelok* are survivors in this category, and we may speculate from our discussion of them whether such tales could usefully have been called romances. There are two other important factors in the discussion. One is that for the first half of the period to 1300 at least, the dominant literary language in England was Anglo-Norman, and since romance is in origin essentially an aristocratic form, such romances as may have been written in England would have been in French. There is plenty of evidence for a lively and very good tradition of Anglo-Norman romance. The other factor— for the moment more relevant—is evidence of a knowledge of romance and the romance style in early vernacular English works of different *genres*.

Thus, in the most important English prose work of this period, the *Ancren Riwle* or *Ancrene Wisse*, a devotional manual for anchoresses, composed in the West Midlands about 1200, there are many incidental images borrowed from

[16] R. M. Wilson, *The Lost Literature of Medieval England* (London, 1952), p. 114

the theory and practice of chivalry. In his use of the ancient allegory of God as a king wooing the soul as bride, the author is clearly influenced by the conventions of chivalric romance: as Geoffrey Shepherd says:

'The king becomes a royal knight; the soul, the highborn lady of romance who is disposed to receive the polite and passionate advances of the lover with disdain.'[17]

Again, the debate poem, *The Owl and the Nightingale*, written between 1189 and 1216, includes a story which may well have been a reminiscence of one of the courtly *lais* of Marie de France. The owl uses the story to show how the nightingale is notorious for leading wives into sin. In Marie de France's *Laustic* the lady conceals her affair with a knightly lover by pretending to her husband that she goes out at night only to listen to the nightingale's song. The husband catches the bird and gives the dead body to his wife, who sends it to her lover as a sign that the relationship must end. The lover treasures it as a precious relic for the rest of his life.[18] Here, then, is another tale of sentimental knightly adultery known to and used by an English poet. But perhaps the most striking evidence of all is contained in Layamon's *Brut*, written between 1189 and 1205, which is a free verse paraphrase of Wace's rhymed chronicle of British history, *Le Roman de Brut*. Wace's handling of his historical material does show signs of a 'romance' influence. The atmosphere of his poem is courtly, and he treats love-episodes in a fashion it is fair to call romantic. Now Layamon is generally hostile to Wace's courtly and romantic treatment of the British epic, and in his paraphrase, he alters the emphasis very considerably. The dominant sentiment of his poem is a fierce patriotism and he restores to the material much of its original epic quality. Nevertheless he reveals an ability to understand and transmit Wace's courtliness when he thinks it appropriate, and, though his direction is overwhelmingly epic, he adds to and amplifies some of Wace's romance motifs.

Two passages in particular stand out: the first being the account of Arthur's begetting by Uther on Ygaerne, the wife of the Earl of Cornwall. Wace gives quite a sophisticated account of Uther's infatuation with Ygaerne, and Layamon, though the subject-matter is not one he finds sympathetic, succeeds largely in

[17] G. Shepherd (ed.), *Ancrene Wisse* pts 6 and 7 (Nelson's Medieval and Renaissance Library, London, 1959), p. 55. The passage occurs on p. 21, line 1ff.
[18] *The Owl and the Nightingale*, ed. E. G. Stanley (Nelson's Medieval and Renaissance Library, London, 1960), lines 1043–66. Marie de France's *lai* of *Laustic* is in Marie de France, *Lais*, ed. A. Ewert (Oxford, 1944). The *lai* form and its relation to the romance is discussed below (pp. 37–8). Marie de France wrote in the last third of the twelfth century: the *lais* appear to have been composed before 1189 and may have been dedicated to King Henry II.

preserving the courtly veneer.[19] A little later, it is true, he cuts down Uther's description of his sufferings for love to the bare minimum:

> 'Ulfin raed me sumne raed other Ich beo ful rathe daede,
> Swa swithe me longe that ne mai I noht libben
> After there faire Igaerne.' (1627–9: Wace 8657–67)

In Wace, Uther can neither sleep nor wake, eat nor drink, rise nor go to bed without thinking of Ygaerne. This elaboration of detail is typical of the courtly romance, and Wace also makes use of the convention of the lover's being 'conquered' and 'taken prisoner' by the lady. Layamon makes the essential point but loses the sophisticated elaboration of it. However, the situation is reversed in a comparison of the respective accounts of Ulfin's advice to Arthur. In Wace, the counsellor says simply that making war on her husband and laying waste his land is hardly the way to win Ygaerne's land. He has no constructive advice to give, except that Uther should seek help from Merlin. Layamon has Ulfin repeat these arguments, but gives him some additional practical suggestions: this time it is the English poet who approximates more closely to courtly romance conventions:

> 'Ah yif thu luvest Igaerne thu sculdest hit halden derne,
> And sende hire sone of seolvere and of golde
> And luvien hire mid liste and mid leofliche bihaeste.' (1641–3)

Here are two of the usual concomitants of *fine amour*, secrecy and devoted service, and possibly a third, if *liste* means 'art' here, rather than 'cunning'. Paradoxically, what suggests most strongly that Layamon was influenced by the courtly convention is that Ulfin's advice turns out to be quite irrelevant. Ygaerne's virtue is impregnable, and Uther sleeps with her through Merlin's stratagem of giving him her husband's likeness, not as a reward for obeying the rules. But Layamon, translating piece by piece, comes to a situation which seems to him to require this kind of treatment, and so he attempts to supply it. He does this again, in telling the story of Arthur's fight against the giant of Mont St Michel. This fight is practically the only romantic feat of arms in the story: all other encounters are of an epic nature. It ought, therefore, to be a fair test of Layamon's knowledge of, or attitude towards, the courtly convention. Though his treatment of the episode is by no means consistent, there are two interesting pieces of detail. He gives Bedver, Arthur's companion, a speech expressing the knightly attitude towards women (the giant has raped and killed a lady, and Bedver meets her nurse bewailing her) and he makes Arthur,

[19] This material can be found most conveniently in *Selections from Layamon's 'Brut'*, ed. G. L. Brook (Clarendon Medieval and Tudor Series, Oxford, 1963). See lines 1531–40. Wace's *Roman de Brut* is edited by I. Arnold (Paris, 1938–40). See lines 8587–96

when he comes across the giant asleep, refrain from taking advantage of him because of a code of honour resembling the chivalric one.[20] There are, then, signs that Layamon has attempted to adapt himself to the telling of a chivalric and romantic story, though these attempts are sporadic, and a digression from the real direction of the poem.

The general conclusions to be drawn from this are as follows: Layamon is a translator, into a language which at that time could be considered as the language of the vulgar in contrast with French. We might be tempted to deduce from this that his treatment of the material would be a popular debasement of it. This is in fact not so: Layamon cannot usefully be called a popular poet. The difficulty is that the chivalric romance is a French invention, and the terms which eventually passed into our language and which we use today to discuss the convention are French terms. It is worth asking whether this may not be the ultimate reason for a critic's calling Layamon's or other Middle English poets' handling of courtly themes primitive or naïve. And is not the question of the relative suitability of French and English as media for the convention quite irrelevant unless it can be proved that an English poet such as Layamon did not understand the French words and the motive behind them? In the above passages, such proof is impossible, but the question will have to be asked again in considering some of the other English poems selected.

The Anglo-Norman Romances

The chivalric romance is most significantly represented in twelfth and thirteenth-century England by Anglo-Norman poems. The most recent criticism of Anglo-Norman literature[21] has demonstrated clearly our error in supposing that Anglo-Norman culture in this period lagged behind that of continental France, and there are a number of romances whose dates correspond quite closely with Chrétien de Troyes' period of productivity—even one or two which may be contemporary with the earliest 'classical' romances. The *Tristan* romances of Thomas and Béroul come from about this period, but in spite of a certain courtliness of treatment, it is questionable whether the essential motivation of the love-affair between Tristan and Iseult or the ideals of conduct evoked correspond to those of medieval chivalric romance. This is, of course, no reflection on the excellence of these poems. They are romances by virtue of their subject of love among the aristocracy, the mixture of this with knightly adventure and (to some extent) by atmosphere. There is, on the other hand, no abstract consideration of the knightly ethic, nor is this ethic freed from realistic considerations. Adultery is a live moral issue here, not a

[20] Lines 25795–26110 in the edition of F. Madden (London, 1847)
[21] M. Dominica Legge, *Anglo-Norman Literature and its Background* (Oxford, 1963)

necessary assumption, and the story is tragic in a way which the true romance cannot be. More relevant are the romances of the Norman-Welsh clerk, Hue de Rotelande, who wrote, between 1174 and 1191, the *Ipomedon* and its sequel, *Protheselaus*. The names, and to some extent, the settings, suggest the typical interest in classical and Byzantine stories, and the use made of the theme of *fine amour* is more orthodox and relevant than is the case in the Tristan romances. Further, especially in the *Ipomedon*, Hue is offering us almost a burlesque of the *genre*: as Miss Legge says,

'His attitude towards romance may be compared with that of the author of *Aucassin* or of Jehan Renart. There is the same quizzical view of elegant society, the same amusement at the behaviour of the young, the same descent into fabliau-esque.' (p. 88)

He appears immensely well-informed about the form he parodies, and it is a striking testimony to its establishment that parody was possible at so early a date, although we look in vain for a comparable tone in English vernacular romance until the fourteenth century.

Perhaps the most distinctively Anglo-Norman romances are those which use for their subject-matter tales from 'The Matter of England', that is, English traditions and legends which the Normans had adopted. The earliest of these is the *Horn et Rimel* of Master Thomas, which provides at least a partial basis for the English *King Horn* discussed below. There is also *Waldef*, and two thirteenth century examples are *Gui de Warewic* and *Boeve de Haumtone*, both of which proved immensely popular (there are extant fourteenth-century English versions of each). The distinctive quality of the last three mentioned stems from their being 'ancestral romances'. Miss Legge defines this term for us thus:

'They were all apparently written to lend prestige to a family which, for one reason or another, could be regarded as parvenu. The hero is regarded as the founder of a family, and must preferably be a king, or become one at the end of the story. There must be a period of exile, if possible involving wanderings over sea, with mention of exotic places, their fauna, and other details. . . . The author may take an existing story and adapt it to his needs, or create a new one, or he may make use of genuine history. Whether his fable is derived from truth or fiction, he will ornament it with signs and wonders. At least one fight with a dragon is almost *de rigueur*. The burial of the hero in a monastery is almost universal. *Courtoisie* finds little place, and only lip-service is paid to it. Since the object of writing at all seems to be to describe the founding of a family, marriage is bound to play an important part; love-affairs outside matrimony are out of place.' (p. 174)

From her account, the relationship of these poems to the notions of romance previously discussed becomes clear. Essentially, they are much more closely engaged with reality, and their chivalry, their attitude to love, is not conceived in abstract terms. Their quality as romance is marginal, a matter of the manner of description and the setting, and of the choice of incident, rather than of tone or meaning. When *fine amour* is treated (as it is at length in *Gui de Warewic*) it is in the conventional terms, but the point is that this love is not an end in itself. Nor is the career of knightly adventure. The theme of a poem like *Gui de Warewic* is not dissimilar from that of the true chivalric romance: it is one of self-realization through love and deeds of arms, thus paralleling, for example, the movement of Chretien's *Yvain*. But the context is different—that is to say, the action exists in a context which the author thinks relevant. There is no context in the chivalric romance proper except what is created by the chivalric ethic itself. In these poems, then, the romance elements are a means of treating certain story-matter, not a way of seeing experience, and the poems come closer to our modern conception of romance as an attractive but not really relevant fiction, which may be enjoyed on an unphilosophic level, simply as entertaining narrative, or, on the other hand, as a style which may clothe and make palatable some other serious concern, as in *Gui de Warewic*. In this, they are close to several of the English poems to be discussed.

The English Romances and their Audience

King Horn, as was previously mentioned, derives almost certainly from a poem in French. This is typical of English romance: there are very few English examples which can be shown to be of purely English genesis. And this makes for one of their distinguishing features: the English romances, in the vast majority of cases, are popular adaptations of French or Anglo-Norman poems written for a more sophisticated audience. In discussing Layamon, I suggested that this argument did not have universal application, but the marks of popularization are widespread and undeniable. Consider some romance openings:

> 'Alle beon he blithe
> That to my song lythe.
> A sang Ihc schal you singe
> Of Murry the kinge.' (*King Horn*)

> 'Herkneth to me, gode men,
> Wives, maydnes, and alle men,
> Of a tale Ich you wil telle,
> Hwoso it wile here and therto duelle.' (*Havelok*)

In the second example, the narrator is not even trying to pretend that his

audience is composed of lords and ladies,[22] and what seems to be suggested is
that the narrator is in the open air, trying to gather an audience round him in
the market-place, and well aware that if he can't catch their attention quickly
they will not 'duelle' but will wander off to buy their eggs and butter. It would
not, of course, be true to suggest that none of the French poems was composed
by a strolling minstrel, but in England, anyway, the language situation would
generally confine the performance of such poems to the halls of the upper
classes. This is clear enough from the texts of the Anglo-French poems that
survive. The first romances of all were literary products, and were made, more
often than not, for a small and select audience, consisting largely of ladies, and
might be read aloud, either by their author, or by a clerk employed for the
purpose, or by one of the ladies (though private reading would also be common). So, at the coronation-feast with which *Havelok* ends, one of the diver-
sions listed is 'Romanz-reding on the bok' and here it is clear enough that the
poet mentions it as an example of 'high life' with which to impress an unsophisticated audience. A clearer picture is given in Chaucer's *Troilus and Criseyde*,
where Pandarus enters Criseyde's house,

> 'And fond two other ladys sete, and she,
> Withinne a paved parlour, and they thre
> Herden a mayden reden hem the geste
> Of the siege of Thebes, while hem leste.'[23]

With these things in mind, we can recognize that the adaptation of romances
to suit public delivery to a popular audience will entail considerable changes of
treatment. The narrative line must be emphasized, at the expense of elaboration
of detail in description (though this still remains an important feature) and
more especially at the expense of the kind of psychological analysis of the motives of love and honour which characterizes the best of the chivalric romances.
The idealistic basis of chivalry, if it remains at all, has to be reinterpreted, often
by poets who do not understand its subtleties, for an audience which would
not understand them either. The texture becomes coarser and looser.

Classifications of Romance: Social, Metrical, etc.

While it would clearly be desirable to make some general classifications in the
body of English Medieval Romance, the task, on inspection, proves to be an

[22] Note Chaucer's ridicule of this pretence in *Sir Thopas*, lines 179–80,
'Now holde youre mouth, *par charitee*/ Bothe knyght and lady free'. See
Ruth Crosby, 'Oral Delivery in the Middle Ages', *Speculum*, xi (1936), pp.
88–110

[23] *Troilus*, ii. 80–4, in *The Complete Works of Geoffrey Chaucer*, ed. F. N.
Robinson (Cambridge, Mass., 1957)

extremely difficult one. The above discussion may have suggested that the social criteria might do: we can ask whether these poems were addressed to a popular, bourgeois, or aristocratic audience. But complications are soon apparent. In the case of early romances like *King Horn*, *Havelok* and *Floriz and Blauncheflur* there is a convenient and sufficiently true equation to be made between popularization and adaptation from the French. Yet over the next hundred and fifty years, the improvement in the literary status of the English vernacular tends to invalidate such an equation. *Sir Gawain and the Green Knight* derives in all probability from French material, but is surely a refinement of it: Chaucer's romances, too, will stand comparison with any French or Italian work. But to say that England by the end of the fourteenth century was capable of refined examples of the chivalric romance is not to deny that the form characteristically manifested itself in the work of popular hacks and translators. Popularization is itself an ambiguous word in this context. There is a clear difference between a sophisticated aristocratic romance which has been simplified, or even debased to suit the needs and understanding of a popular audience, and a poem which has been deliberately put together out of the tastes and attitudes of such an audience and borrows the form of the romance for reasons of convenience and literary prestige. It is the distinction that should be made between *King Horn* and *Havelok*, for example. We should be clear also that this concept of popularization has only a limited critical relevance. Of course, it is likely that, the romance being the subtle and aristocratic form that it is, popularization will impoverish the philosophical ethos of the poem, will fail to preserve the theme of spiritual education in the hero, and will leave us, at best, with a lavishly described account of picturesque adventures to justify its title of romance. But this impoverishment is not necessarily in proportion with the popular nature of the treatment. If the definitions of romance proposed in this essay are valid, they are so only in terms of their critical usefulness—that is to say, according to whether or not their use releases to us the energy of a particular poem. If it does not, the literary historian may still find much of interest in the poem in terms of the romance convention, but his value-judgments should be made in other terms. And, in the last analysis, the social criteria play only a secondary part in this. The question, what is a romance? has to do with a poem's theme, its meaning, not primarily with its style, or the audience to whom it is addressed. Unless we get our categories right on these issues, it is vain to attach much critical importance to the secondary ones. A crude, vulgar piece of hack-work like *Beves of Hamtoun* does require to be judged as a romance: a comparatively highly-wrought and sophisticated heroic epic like the alliterative *Morte Arthure* of the Thornton MS. does *not*— it isn't a romance in spite of the bibliographies. A vague feeling that an Arthurian theme, a share of marvellous happenings and a good deal of elaborately sophisticated description make a chivalric romance won't do.

The choice of subject-matter is a little more reliable as a guide. Of course there are certain time-honoured situations which are cited as archetypal for Epic and Romance: Ker's 'defence of a narrow place against odds' and '(the) collision of blind forces, (the) tournament at random (which) takes the place . . . of the older form of combat' (pp. 5, 6).[24] The literary historian can trace recurrent plots and situations in the body of the English romances and tell us much about the compositional relationship between them. But again the exercise has limited critical value. Let us use the *Morte Arthure* again, as an example. There is another, roughly contemporary English poem on this theme, *Le Morte Arthur* of the Harley MS. Though the basic narrative outline of Arthur's death is common to both, the poems represent two different Arthurian traditions: the primitive epic version, and the courtly romance modification of it. Though in *Le Morte Arthur* something of the heroic quality does inhere in the situation itself, a critic will be forced to acknowledge its essential nature as romance, in contrast with the alliterative poem. Romance requires a significant union of *matière* and *sen*, which is not likely to come about accidentally through an unthinking rehearsal of story-matter, unless that story-matter has been consciously adapted to the romance convention in a previous recension.

Perhaps the most useful classification, however, is the metrical one (which means leaving the prose romances, which are a fifteenth-century phenomenon in England, out of the reckoning). This gives us three classes: romances in rhyming couplets (generally four-beat); those in tail-rhyme stanza or a variant of it; and the alliterative romances. What generalizations are possible about these classes? The octosyllabic couplet, of course, is intimately connected with the development of romance in France, serving, indeed, as one of the distinguishing marks of the form. The earliest English romances use it inevitably, though the couplet of *King Horn* derives from the influence of the French couplet on the native alliterative line, as illustrated in the metre of Layamon's *Brut*. Auerbach has much of critical importance to say on the change from the *laisse* of the *chanson de geste* with its characteristically paratactic movement to the 'hypotactically richer and more periodic syntax' of the couplet romances.[25] He characterizes the style of the *chanson de geste* thus:

'The poet explains nothing; and yet the things which happen are stated with a paratactic bluntness which says that everything must happen as it does happen, it could not be otherwise, and there is no need for explanatory

---

[24] For an interesting criticism of Ker's argument see D. M. Hill, 'Romance as Epic', *English Studies*, xliv (1963), 95–107

[25] The terms 'parataxis' and 'hypotaxis' perhaps merit a note. In paratactic syntax, statements are juxtaposed without grammatical connexion of the kind that hypotactic syntax supplies.

connectives. This, as the reader knows, refers not only to the events but also to the views and principles which form the basis of the actions of the persons concerned.' (p. 88)

In the couplet-form, the fluidity, the ease of movement and loose connexions influence the experimental nature of the romance experience. The hero is freed by this neutral style from the hieratic gesture of the *duzepers*: he is enabled to set out on his individual search for self-knowledge. But, as Auerbach himself reminds us, the couplet serves the most varied ends, and it is doubtful whether its employment in the earliest English romances signifies anything more precise than the general influence of French metrics on the English of the period. The couplet appears to have yielded to the tail-rhyme stanza as the popular medium for English romances during the fourteenth century: though four of Chaucer's five romances are in decasyllabic couplets, it is notable that the burlesque *Sir Thopas* exploits the tail-rhyme. Nevertheless, couplets go on being used, as the most common narrative metre, and enjoy something of a revival in the surviving fifteenth-century romances. It is not really possible to assign the use of the couplet to any particular area or areas of the country.

With the tail-rhyme romances, however, this assignation may be attempted. There is disagreement in detail about the localization of individual poems, but we shall be safe in saying the eastern half of the country, and fairly safe in specifying the East Midlands, though a number of the later examples come from further north, and Trounce argued long and hard for an East Anglian origin.[26] The origins of the stanza seem to have been in Latin church poetry, but it is difficult to be certain whether it came into English direct from hymns in the *versus tripertiti caudati*, or from a French modification of that form. The latter is suggested by the terms of Robert Mannyng's attack (*c.* 1330) on new-fangled rhyming metres:

> 'If it were made in *ryme couwee*,
>   Or in strangere, or enterlace,
>   That rede Inglis it ere inowe
>   That couthe not haf coppled a kowe,
>   That outhere in *couwee* òr in *baston*
>   Som suld haf ben fordon.'[27]

The remarkable feature of its use in English is its popularity as a metre for romance. Out of forty-six surviving poems employing a version of the tail-

---

[26] A. McI. Trounce, 'The English Tail-Rhyme Romances', *M.Æ.*, i (1932), 87–108, 168–82; ii (1933), 34–57, 189–98; iii (1934), 30–50

[27] *Robert Mannyng of Brunne's Chronicle*, ed. F. J. Furnivall (Rolls Series, London, 1887), i. 85–90

rhyme strophe, or whose metrics can be related to it, thirty-three are romances.[28] In Latin on the other hand, it is essentially a lyric, not a narrative measure. It does not appear at all in surviving narrative poetry, though a little is found in the drama. Its use in French also is in general limited to serious religious works, though it appears as a narrative measure in hagiographic poems, in Langtoft's *Chronicle* and in the drama. No romance in tail-rhyme survives. How, then, can we explain its popularity in England as a romance metre—a popularity which extends from the late thirteenth century into the fifteenth? At first sight it would seem completely unsuited for sustained narrative, but when we consider that medieval poetry in general was designed for a listening rather than a reading public, the choice seems more reasonable. On the whole, these poems appear to be designed for a popular audience, though one extending to a relatively cultivated bourgeoisie and excluding the totally unsophisticated, and they are the work of professional commercial writers, usually of fair competence. It is easy enough to see the suitability of the tail-rhyme stanza for public recitation: the simple and strongly-marked rhythm would aid reciter and listener alike to retain the thread of the narrative, while it is also a metre which lends itself to a species of oral composition depending on the accumulation of conventional formulae and phrases. Very often, the tail-rhyme romances are highly alliterative, and preserve many of the words and tags of the Old English poetic tradition. In two of the romances selected, *Sir Thopas* and *Sir Degrevant*, we see the respective failures and successes of this reliance on a conventional store of poetic diction. These are perhaps the most likely reasons for the widespread popularity of the metre in the English romance: one wonders why the reasons for it rejection—more cogent to us—did not prevail. It is monotonous—so is the couplet, but its monotony is not as obtrusive— and it has a strong tendency to fragment. Its stanzaic arrangement would, in any case, seem to militate against narrative fluidity, and the stanza itself is generally composed of distinct three-line units, a couplet followed by a shorter third line, bound together by the same rhyme in the third line of each unit. What are likely to be the literary effects of the use of this stanza in romance? If we look back to Auerbach, we can say, perhaps, that the stanza acts (or should act) in the same way as the *laisse* of the *chanson de geste*, in presenting a series of single poetic events, static, and testifying to the established order, rather than to one which the poem itself seeks out. The form does not aid speculative exploration of a theme in the way the couplet can be said to do. On the whole, this hypothesis is borne out by a study of the existing tail-rhyme romances, and it is interesting to see how many of them have a markedly ortho- dox religious and moral purpose (*Amis and Amiloun* affords some testimony

[28] See C. Strong, 'History and Relations of the Tail-Rhyme Strophe in Latin, French and English', *P.M.L.A.* xxii (1907), 371–417

B

here). But besides this, most are more or less competent rehashes of conventional plot-motifs, and are romances by virtue of this, and of their atmospheric qualities, rather than by their explorations of the chivalric experience. There are exceptions, of which *Sir Degrevant* is one of the most notable, where the kind of audience addressed has clearly had some effect on the poet's treatment of the theme, where the courtly ethic is modified to suit bourgeois taste, yet still remains distinctly alive. What, finally, the tail-rhyme tradition suggests is a flourishing and respectable literary industry.

The third metrical category is made up of the dozen or so alliterative 'romances'. The traditional localization of the poetry of the alliterative revival in the North and West Midland is beginning to be challenged, but these poems as a group offer no clear evidence either way. Two of them, *William of Palerne* and *Joseph of Arimathie*, are dated about 1350, and are thus the earliest examples of the alliterative revival that survive: some of the others may be as much as a hundred years later. If we look at the subject-matter and themes of the group, we find that five poems are Arthurian, with Gawain playing a prominent part in three of them—*Sir Gawain and the Green Knight*, *The Awntyrs of Arthur* and *Golagros and Gawain*. We can relate this to the general popularity of Gawain in English medieval romance: he was never really replaced by Lancelot as the pre-eminent Arthurian hero in this country, except in the prose of Malory. Further, there seems to have been something of a cult of Gawain in the North and West: most of the dozen surviving Gawain romances, including these three, appear to come from there. The other interesting feature of the group is that it contains a large body of pseudo-historical epic material—the *Alliterative Alexander Fragments*, *The Destruction of Troy* and *The Destruction of Jerusalem*. *The Destruction of Troy* in particular, as can be seen from the Prologue which is excerpted below, sets great store on authenticity, and appears to be critical of the new-fangled inventions of the writers of romance. The predominance of the epic amongst these works is further emphasized when we remember that one of the Arthurian poems is the heroic *Morte Arthure*. Nevertheless, generalizations about the group's specific character are very dangerous. If it contains substantial epics, it also contains the supreme English example of the chivalric romance in *Sir Gawain and the Green Knight*: if it is elegantly sophisticated here, and learned in the *Destruction of Troy*, it is popular and boisterous in *The Awntyrs of Arthur*. The alliterative poems have been seen as a nationalistic gesture, or as a revolt of the provinces against London culture,[29] yet they generally use French or Latin sources, and the art of a poem like *Sir Gawain* can in no very useful sense be called provincial. What we may say, very tentatively, about the effect of alliterative style on 'romance' material is that its

[29] See J. R. Hulbert, 'A Hypothesis Concerning the Alliterative Revival', *MP*, xxviii (1931), 405–22

traditional association with the heroic epic has some effect on the choice of subject-matter: *Sir Gawain and the Green Knight*, not the *Morte Arthure*, is the exceptional achievement in this field.

The Manuscripts of the Romances

In connexion with what was said above concerning the reading and recitation of the English medieval romances, there is perhaps some point in ascertaining what can be learnt from a study of the manuscripts in which they are preserved. What is immediately striking is the high percentage of romances which only exist in a single copy. As long as we remember that there is no knowing how many manuscripts have been lost, we can still use this fact to suggest something about the nature of the form. Most of the surviving romances were popular: they belonged to the repertory of a travelling minstrel who would be far more likely to pride himself on his memory than on his library. If he kept a copy of any of the poems he composed or acquired, it would be only to refresh his memory. The copy would have had hard usage, and cannot have stood a very good chance of physical survival. Moreover, the reciter is not likely to have welcomed the making of copies by his audience: the poems were his livelihood, and must have been jealously guarded. Copies, of course, were made—as Sisam puts it, 'fair closet copies that would have enabled well-to-do admirers to renew their pleasure when no skilled minstrel was by'.[30] Nevertheless, five or six copies seems to have been about the average, even for such popular stories as *Guy of Warwick* or *Beves of Hamtoun*. When we examine a romance which exists in a number of manuscripts, further hazards of the enquiry become apparent. Sisam points out, for example (p. xxxiv), that none of the four copies of *Floriz and Blauncheflur* preserve the beginning of the poem. A minstrel's rehearsal of a romance must have varied to a greater or lesser extent every time he uttered it: as Robert Mannyng complains:

> 'I see in song, in sedgeyng tale
> Of Erceldoun and of Kendale,
> Non tham says as thai tham wroght,
> And in ther sayng it semes noght.
> That may thou here in *Sir Tristrem*—
> Over gestes it has the steem,
> Over alle that is or was,
> If men it sayd as made Thomas:
> But I here it no man so say,
> That of som copple som is away.' (i. 93–102)

It is only rarely (as, perhaps, in the case of the exemplar of the Laud MS of

[30] K. Sisam (ed.), *Fourteenth Century Verse and Prose* (Oxford, 1921), p. xxxiii

Havelock and *King Horn*) that a confident identification of one of the surviving romance manuscripts as a minstrel's copy can be made, or that one can assert that a poem was taken down from recitation. On the other hand, it is clear enough that romances were read as well as listened to, and many of them survive in quite elaborate 'library copies', though these never, in England, attain to the elegance, say, of some of the French manuscripts of *Le Roman de la Rose*. The manuscript of *Sir Gawain and the Green Knight*, for example, has coloured capitals, and four (rather mediocre) illustrations. It is perhaps these, not the poem itself, which suggest provinciality,[31] and the manuscript may be one of the 'fair closet copies' of which Sisam speaks.

The other striking feature which emerges from a study of the romance manuscripts is the existence of a number of anthologies of romance. The most notable, of which this selection makes quite extensive use, is the Auchinleck Manuscript, now in the National Library of Scotland, Edinburgh, in which are found no fewer than eighteen romances, together with a variety of other material. Robert Thornton's manuscript, Lincoln Cathedral MS A.5.2, is also remarkable, and a substantial collection is to be found in the British Museum MS Cotton Caligula A.ii. Among these collections, we can make the following speculative distinctions: those produced commercially in bookshops for sale to amateurs of literature; those made by the amateurs themselves; and those made in monastic communities, where the taste for secular literature never seems to have been eradicated. It has become clear, through the work of Laura Hibbard Loomis,[32] that the Auchinleck Manuscript comes in the first category. It comes from the second quarter of the fourteenth century, is mostly the work of London scribes, and seems to have been produced in a London bookshop. It is pleasantly produced, though not lavish, and the romances, as Mrs Loomis says, 'are of the most varied kind and well-designed to catch all tastes' (p. 606). Its particular interest, besides all this, is its possible connexion with Chaucer, for which Mrs Loomis argues most persuasively. The knowledge of romances which he reveals in his burlesque *Sir Thopas* could well have been supplied out of his reading of the Auchinleck romances, and his particular indebtedness to the two versions of *Guy of Warwick* which it contains strengthens the case. Add to this the close connexion between what he says about the Breton *lai* in

[31] See G. Mathew, 'Ideals of Knighthood in late fourteenth-century England' in *Studies in Medieval History presented to F. M. Powicke*, edd. R. W. Hunt, W. A. Pantin, R. W. Southern (Oxford, 1948), pp. 354–62

[32] L. H. Loomis, 'The Auchinleck MS and a possible London bookshop of 1330–40', *P.M.L.A.*, lvii (1942), 595–627. For the connexion between this MS and Chaucer, see her articles, 'Chaucer and the Breton Lays of the Auchinleck MS', *S.P.* xxxviii (1941), 14–33, and 'Chaucer and the Auchinleck MS' in *Essays and Studies in Honour of Carleton Brown*, ed. P. W. Long (New York, 1940), 111–28

The Franklin's Tale and the Auchinleck *Lai Le Freine* and *Sir Orfeo*, and it seems highly probable that he knew the manuscript, if he did not actually own it.

In the second category comes the Thornton MS. The old idea that Thornton was a churchman and Archdeacon of Bedford has given way to a theory which makes him a Yorkshire country gentleman. In either case, he seems to have had time to indulge his literary hobby, and to have made copies of poems, especially romances, for his own private delectation. The poems in the Thornton MS come from a number of dialect areas, and the processes by which he obtained them must have been complex. We can allot the Cotton MS Caligula A.ii to the third category. The twelve long narrative poems, eight of them romances, which it contains, appear to have been copied by a single scribe between 1446 and 1460. Edith Rickert characterizes the manuscript thus:

> 'From the plain workmanlike character of the MS and its marked religious and didactic element, it would seem to have been a tale-book copied in some monastery.'[33]

King Horn

The brief comments on the selections do not purport to be complete critical accounts of the poems. This is not an anthology of romance, and the passages are chosen to throw some light on specific aspects of the *genre*. At times, the results will be negative: for though all these poems are traditionally classed as romances, several of them are much better talked about in quite other terms: to demonstrate why this is so still seems a valid undertaking.

The two excerpts from *King Horn* make up a total of some 350 lines, which obviously does not give adequate grounds for a criticism of its quality as narrative, which, in the reading of it, is perhaps its main virtue. The first passage says all the poem has to say about medieval chivalric romance, while the second is chosen to illustrate its more vague, more 'modern' romantic quality. It should be clear from the synopsis of the plot given with the text how intractable a subject for medieval romance the story is. Horn is, in fact, engaged in realistic political activity, however much fantasticated it is in the telling. The adventures do not take place in a dreamland, but in a world which seems to derive, however remotely, from the actual historical relations between Britain and Ireland at the time of the Viking domination (the pagan Norsemen have been replaced by the more fashionable Saracen villains of the *chanson de geste* tradition). The whole direction of the narrative is towards Horn's recovery of his kingdom and towards marriage. Marriage, moreover, as presented in this poem, seems very much a matter of politics and economics. The heroine is almost married off

[33] E. Rickert (ed.), *The Romance of Emaré*, E.E.T.S., E.S. 99 (1908), p. xi

twice, against her will, like a piece of property. On the other hand, the story is obviously 'romantic' in the vaguer sense suggested above: the love of Horn and Rymenhild is central to the plot, Horn journeys overseas into strange lands, and turns up in disguise (twice!) in the nick of time to save his mistress—obviously 'romantic' situations, illustrated very well in the second passage. The first, however, has a good deal more to offer. If we look closely at this first meeting of Horn and Rymenhild, we find that though it is she and not Horn who is initially overcome by love, she is at least in a position of power over him, as the king's daughter. This illustrates a fact of feudalism which gave rise to the images of the haughty mistress and suppliant lover of the courtly tradition: in *King Horn*, however, it remains on the level of fact. Horn finds Rymenhild in her chamber surrounded by her maidens, a typical romance situation. Her behaviour, though, is not so typical:

> 'Heo makede him feire chere
> And tok him abute the swere.
> Oft heo him custe,
> So wel so hire luste' (I, 25–8),

and she flatly offers herself as his bride. Horn, however, is a remarkably cool and shrewd young man, and if he feels any emotion at this, neither he nor the poet makes it apparent. He replies:

> 'Ihc am ibore to lowe
> Such wimman to knowe.' (39–40)

This would seem a stock example of the courtly lover's declaration of unworthiness, except that Horn is well aware of his own royal birth, and that he does not argue that he is spiritually unworthy, but socially. Rymenhild faints at this rebuff, and Horn is, it would seem, moved by pity to comfort her and to propose the solution of getting himself knighted by her father, through her intercession. It is hard not to feel, however, that Horn wants above all to be knighted, and is prepared to use Rymenhild's love as a lever to bring this about. Yet this interpretation would in any case pay tribute to the notion of romantic chivalry. When Horn says 'I schal wexe more' (being knighted) there is implicit a belief in the spiritual powers invested in the mystique of chivalry. Horn does not appear to mean that he will be financially better able to support a royal princess in the style to which she is accustomed. And this belief is underlined when, after Horn's dubbing, Rymenhild reopens the question of marriage. Horn now excuses himself by saying that a knight has to prove himself in combat before he can take a wife—'of ure mestere/So is the manere.' Apart, perhaps, from the assumption that married love is the ultimate goal of the knight's endeavour, this is the classic union of the chivalric themes of love and honour. However, this theme is really marginal in the poem as it stands. Horn only undertakes one adventure of this kind, and though his love for Rymenhild remains constant throughout the poem, it is henceforth presented in less sophisticated terms. A further interesting detail in this passage, which testifies in some way to the chivalric ideal, is the ring which Rymenhild gives Horn, saying:

> 'The stones beoth of suche grace,
> That thu ne schalt in none place
> Of none duntes beon ofdrad,
> Neo on bataille beon amad,
> Ef thu loke theran
> And thenke upon thi lemman.' (193–8)

The ring has two significances, and it is hard to tell which is more dominant. On the one hand it is a simple magic talisman: certain powers inhere in the stones of the ring. On the other, it symbolizes the love-motif: *if* Horn looks upon it, he will be reminded of his mistress, and it is this memory which will give him strength. What needs to be said finally about *King Horn* in the context of this book is that its preoccupations are not essentially those of the chivalric romance, but that, though it is in all likelihood a popularized and simplified translation from a more sophisticated French poem, it does reveal marginally an awareness of what the chivalric romance is about. It is not *positively* unsophisticated or uncourtly.

Havelok

In contrast to *King Horn*, *Havelok* appears a consciously popular poem, and the difference between them is indicated by comparison of their opening lines quoted above (p. 20). Even more than *Horn*, *Havelok* is a fiction arising out of a real political situation: the union of the English and Danish kingdoms in the late Old English period. Indeed, there is quite a plausible connexion between the hero and the tenth-century Viking leader, Olafr Cuaran. The poem also has strong local associations with Lincolnshire. Grim, Havelok's foster-father, is the legendary founder of Grimsby, and the poet, who writes in the local dialect, clearly knows Lincoln very well. The poem is thus strongly anchored by time and place to a real world, and this is apparent in the treatment. It is, nonetheless, a 'romantic' story, and romantic in a very familiar way. It retains the flavour of the 'local boy makes good' kind of folk-tale, allowing to its audience a very easy piece of wish-fulfilment in the account of the hero's fortunes. It may be argued that this cannot be so, since Havelok is a royal prince, but in fact his birth is simply part of the poem's machinery: it is not employed consciously as an explanation of his prowess or as a significant factor in the presentation of his character. Horn was also a foundling and in service, but he was always conscious of his true status and naturally assumed the leadership of his band of companions. Havelok, on the other hand, is a charming simpleton. He seems to have virtually no intimations of his greatness until halfway through the poem, when, his bride having explained his prophetic dream to him, he remembers his childhood. He appears to be perfectly fulfilled in his humble station, first as a fisherman's boy and then as a scullion. His lack of ambition is well illustrated in the first passage selected. In the surviving French version of the story, Grim sends the boy away to the city because he does not feel that fishing is a suitable occupation for a king's son, but in the English poem, though this motive is probably implicit, in that Grim always has greater concern for Havelock than for his own family, the explicit motive is economic necessity.

Havelok has the usual qualities of the hero of folk-tale, and though most of them would be shared by the hero of the chivalric romance, they are here illustrated in non-chivalric circumstances—his kindness and generosity is manifest in his readiness to play with children, for example. At the stone-putting, he takes no part until he is ordered to do so by his master the cook, of whom he is 'sore adrad': hardly ever in the poem does he act out of an awareness of his natural superiority. The love-theme is largely taken for granted. It is not a significant force in the poem, and it is interesting to note, in the second extract, the attitude of Earl Ubbe towards Goldeboru. She is a desirable possession of Havelok's, and Ubbe fears that the villains may kill her 'louerd' in order to possess her. When Havelok fights, as shown in this extract, he behaves as a true hero, but his modes of procedure are hardly orthodox. He takes on the sixty robbers with the bar of a door, and his foster-brothers join in with similar homely weapons. The poet describes the fight with an almost comic relish, the dominant image being of men chastising naughty boys, and Havelok's brothers comment on the action with something of the dour wit of the Icelandic sagas. The rewards which Havelok doles out at the end of the poem are of a highly material kind—land and women—and the mystique of knighthood is in no way evoked here. He is the ideal hero of the people, rooted in the world in which they live (the most vivid passages in the poem are those which show Grim and Havelok going about their everyday business), but miraculously brought from rags to riches. It is a very lively and successful piece of escape literature, but testifies not at all to the ideals of the knightly classes. If it is at all influenced by a notion of chivalric romance, it is only by the superficial attractiveness of the form.

Floriz and Blauncheflur

In this poem we come much nearer to the characteristic concerns and qualities of romance. There is no question here of a realistic political situation, and the only factual element is perhaps the heavily embroidered account of the city of Babylon. This setting, of course, is chosen for its exotic and 'romantic' quality. The poem deals with the love of a Saracen boy and a Christian girl—a love which overcomes all opposition. Further, this love is presented in a highly emotional and sentimental fashion, as the first extract, describing Floriz's grief at the supposed death of his 'friend', bears witness. It is a poem full of luxury and artifice, even in this popular English version (popular in the manner of *King Horn*, not of *Havelok*), which has had to sacrifice much of the detailed elaboration of its sophisticated French predecessor, and the action is almost completely divorced from realistic considerations. In atmosphere, *Floriz and Blauncheflur* would seem perhaps the closest English approach to the sophisticated love-romances of the courtly tradition.

Yet it is necessary to insist that the poem is not essentially a *medieval* romance: it has nothing to say about feudal chivalry, nor is it an account of the hero's spiritual education. The love described is not *fine amour*, even though it is handled in a rather similar fashion. The love of the two 'children' (for this is how they are described) is not simply allowed to override all other considerations in the action: it *is* the only consideration, in rather the same way that *fine amour* is the moral imperative of Chrétien's *Lancelot*. However, the two lovers are not in the relationship of mistress and servant; they are two children together against an adult world, and their love is completely mutual. It can hardly be adulterous, for they are not adults. The poem thus belongs to romance in the same way as the Greek prose romances which may have given rise to it. The second passage, describing the wonders of Babylon, does, nevertheless, exemplify the medieval romance's atmosphere of wonder—a wonder which manifests itself in the face of Oriental plumbing, as well as more supernatural aspects of the scene.

Sir Orfeo

The implications of *Sir Orfeo's* claim to be a Breton *lai* are discussed below (pp. 37–8). It is generally agreed to be one of the best of the English romances, and its particular relevance to our discussion of medieval romance lies in its evocation of the fairy world. In this, it is interesting to see the adaptation of the classical myth of a descent into the world of the dead into the terms of medieval and Celtic mythology. The fairies are quite unlike those of Miss Enid Blyton: they are cold, sinister and powerful beings, and the poem gains its effect from the contrast between their chill menace and the warmth of human sentiment displayed by the three earthlings, Orfeo, Heurodis and the steward.[34] This contrast is most strikingly illustrated in the arbitrary (and irrelevant) violence of the Fairy King's threat to Heurodis that if she does not come with him willingly, she will be fetched:

[34] *cf.* G. Kane, *Middle English Literature* (London, 1951), p. 81

B*

'And yif thou makest ous y-let,
Whar thou be, thou worst y-fet,
And to-tore thine limes al,
That nothing help the ne schal.' (IV. 155–8)

And when Orfeo follows the fairy host into the rock and sees the fairy castle before him in all its hard, bright splendour, he sees also a grim tableau of violent death. The evocation of the fairy atmosphere is not consistent, for as well as this jewel-like clarity, there is, in the descriptions of the appearance of the fairy hosts to Orfeo in the woods, a more expected (to a modern mind, at least) insubstantial, phantom-like quality. No doubt, though, it is pedantic to expect fairies to be consistent.

The general effect of the poem, then, is one fairly characteristic of romance and epic—the definition of human goodness by the presence of a power that is other than human. It has a romantic atmosphere, and is, in fact, one of the few medieval romances that a modern reader would be inclined to call 'romantic'. Its plot, supra-rational, and exhibiting a sympathetic treatment of human love in the marriage relationship, and with a happy ending, is of the class of the Greek prose romances, or of Shakespeare's last plays. It also illustrates, to some extent, the medieval romance writer's treatment of a myth. The classical story of Orpheus and Eurydice is amputated, and a happy ending substituted, which certainly seems to argue against the presence in the poem of the original mythic power of the legend. Orfeo's skill as a harper is largely dwelt on to advertise the story-teller's own wares. The story is brought into a contemporary setting and thoroughly medievalized, with Thrace turning out to be the old name for Winchester. It lacks, however, any sense of chivalric values and ideals, and though the hero undergoes much suffering in the course of the story, this simply testifies to the power of his devotion and is not related to any scheme of self-realization.

Amis and Amiloun

This poem represents the level of solid technical competence attained by the best of the English tail-rhyme romances: as MacEdward Leach says in the introduction to his edition:

'The twelve-line stanza functions here usually as the vehicle for a single episode, or scene, or situation. The result is that each stanza is a definite narrative unit, with a transitional opening, a development and a conclusion. Although this makes for a marked interruption in the flow of narrative, and accounts for an impression of jerkiness in style, yet there is a distinct gain over the non-stanzaic forms of verse, for example, in dramatic intensity and vividness.' (p. xcix)

The argument is exaggerated, in the last clause, but holds. It also suggests the most striking feature of this poem in relation to the central argument, for *Amis and Amiloun* is governed by—is written to illustrate—a single concept, that of sworn brotherhood, which acts as a moral imperative in the poem. It makes Amiloun undertake an unjust quarrel to defend Amis, even though he is warned he will be smitten by leprosy for it, and it makes Amis, in the passage excerpted, slay his children to heal his brother. This dogma of sworn brotherhood is the *sen* of *Amis and Amiloun*, and the stanza, in presenting a series of static and exemplary gestures, testifies to the established order. This is the poem's strength: its weakness is that the poet is not satisfied with it, and tries spasmodically to infuse a quality of realism into his ideal situation. Thus, Amis's furtive preparations for the killing of his children have a local dramatic effectiveness, but hardly persuade us of the justice of the sacrifice. The poet gives Amiloun a prophetic dream, foretelling he can be cured by the blood of his brother's children, which matches Amis's own vision, but then he does nothing with it, so that Amiloun's grief and horror at the killing fails in conviction. The heroine, Belisaunt, who is so vivid and forceful a character in the earlier parts of the poem—in the course of her seduction of Amis, she tells the reluctant hero 'Thou schust have ben a frere'—is reduced to a featureless upholder of the poem's morality. *Amis and Amiloun*, then, has a governing idea, as chivalric romance ought to have, and a number of potentially interesting human situations, which are imperfectly synchronized. The concept of brotherhood, though it coincides well enough with the chivalric ideal, is not specifically connected with it, for Amis and Amiloun have taken their oath before they are dubbed. The story is 'romantic' and relies heavily on the supernatural, but its quality as chivalric romance is not much more than a top-dressing. It is significant that the story seems to have been originally cast in the form of a *chanson de geste*, and that many of its derivatives are hagiography.

The Destruction of Troy

This poem is not a romance, in spite of the bibliographies, and the presence of its prologue in this book is largely self-explanatory. The poet sees his task as that of a chronicler: the historical integrity of the material is all-important, and poets have no right to invent, or impress their own interpretation on the events. He expresses a preference for old 'true' tales of 'auncetris nobill' and disparages new fictions, in terms which suggest a rudimentary critical distinction between the historical epic and romance. Romance as a literary form begins, it is true, in French adaptations of classical epic, like the *Roman de Troie*, from which this derives at second-hand, but the English poet shows little interest in the romantic possibilities of his sources. He rises from chronicler to poet in those scenes where he is able to match his heroic alliterative line to violent happenings.

Sir Thopas

Predictably, the poem in this book which tells us most about the chivalric romance is the one which parodies the *genre*. *Sir Thopas* has everything that the chivalric romance ought to have—except sense. I want to concentrate here on its positive aspect, since its satirical intentions are indicated in the notes on the text, but one or two general remarks can be made. Two satirical purposes have been identified in the poem, neither of them exclusive of the other. The first is obvious: to expose to ridicule the shortcomings of the popular romance, or even of romance as a literary form. The second, suggested by J. M. Manly,[35] who is sceptical about the first, is to satirize the pretensions to chivalry of the Flemish magnates, Jacob and Philip van Artevelde, who, he says, 'were treated by French and English alike with patrician superciliousness as *nouveaux riches*' (p. 60). While not denying the likelihood of this topical reference, I cannot feel that it accounts for the poem's total effect. There is a self-conscious delight in the mastery of a literary form far in excess of what might be needed to demolish Philip van Artevelde. But is Chaucer satirizing popular romance, or merely writing a burlesque? It is not a question which admits of a final answer. His choice of the tail-rhyme stanza, whose limitations are so cruelly exposed, may have been determined by no particular animus against it, but by the simple fact that it was the most popular medium for romance in the England of his day. He wrote serious romances himself (though never, it is true, with an unambiguous acceptance of chivalric conventions) and, as George Kane says, 'accepted the *genre* as legitimate and as one in which success was possible' (p. 55).

Sir Thopas can best be seen by the modern reader as a piece of practical criticism of the chivalric romance, which indicates the faults of the *genre*, but also indicates, by implication, what it was trying to do. Thopas, for example, is the only hero in all the poems in this book who is a true knight-errant, the only one whose whole life is devoted to the pursuit of chivalry. This of itself is not comic, however: if it were, then the poem would be a satire on romance. What is comic about Thopas is that he is not very good at being a knight. He looks wrong, he can't manage a horse, and his natural inclinations are hopelessly bourgeois. The action of the poem has the kind of inconsequential nature, when judged by realistic criteria, that the ideal nature of the romance experience requires. Thopas resolves to fall in love with an elf-queen because that is what knights in romances do: the giant appears because a knight-errant who seeks adventure must find it. These events are ridiculous because the poem establishes no meaningful context for them in terms of the hero's progressive realization of the ideals of chivalry. Instead, a genially hostile and reductive eye is cast upon them. It is this lack of meaning, of a concept governing the

[35] J. M. Manly, '*Sir Thopas*: A Satire', *Essays and Studies*, xiii (1928), 52–73

action, which is the final indictment of the unsuccessful romance. A similar method reveals itself in the style and atmosphere of the poem. The world is an ideal world, filled with bright and varied life, but the colours never quite blend. It is a world full of booby-traps, invested by a booby, who ambles through it at the rocking-horse pace of the tail-rhyme stanza.

Emaré

The decision to include excerpts from a poem which is generally agreed to be of poor quality needs some justification. Like the comic *Sir Thopas*, *Emaré* illustrates the depths of ineptitude to which English medieval romance could sink, and the first passage has been chosen as an example of the common mishandling of the marvellous. The plot, which is a version of the famous 'Constance saga', is, in its vicissitudes, in its theme of happiness lost and found again, romantic in the manner of Shakespeare's last plays. The poem has nothing to do with chivalry; nor are the heroine's sufferings educative, for her virtue is unimprovable. The limit of its success is represented in the second passage, where the pathos of Emaré's situation, cast adrift in an open boat with her infant son, is exploited, though even this, since it duplicates a previous casting-adrift, may be felt to be too much of a good thing. The first passage is largely occupied by a description of the magic cloth, which is subsequently made into a robe for the heroine. The cloth is a love-charm, and should explain the incestuous passion of the Emperor for his daughter, and later, the passion of the King of Galys. This motif, however, is dully rationalized, and the description is a flabby and repetitive attempt to create an atmosphere of material luxury, in which the fragmentary tendency of the tail-rhyme stanza is seen at its worst.

Of more interest is the poem's final assertion:

> Thys ys on of Brytayne layes,
> That was used by olde dayes,
> Men callys "playn the garye". (1030-2)

Two of our poems, then (the other being *Sir Orfeo*), claim this descent, and it is time here for a brief discussion of what they imply. Marie de France is our chief source of information on the Breton *lai* and the poet of *Sir Orfeo* seems likely to have derived his knowledge of the form from her.[36] It is clear from what Marie says that the original Breton *lais* were primarily songs, sung to the harp, and that, as A. J. Bliss points out:

> 'The words were lyrical rather than narrative . . . they expressed the emotions of the hero or heroine on some specific occasion.'[37]

[36] Compare lines 1-24 of *Sir Orfeo* with Marie's *Prologue* 27-42 and *Equitan* 1-8

[37] A. J. Bliss (ed.), *Sir Orfeo* (Oxford, 1954), p. xxviii

But the *lais* frequently referred to a story (*cunte*) which may have been told by the minstrel in order to supply the background necessary for the understanding of his song. The *lais* of Marie herself appear to derive from the *cunte* rather than the *lai*. These two English poems may illustrate the distinction, for while the original of *Sir Orfeo* is likely to have been a narrative poem, what seems to be suggested in the lines from Emaré is a French *Playnt d'Egarye* (*i.e.* 'The Complaint of the Outcast') in which the heroine herself gives lyric expression to her sorrows. The integrity of the *lai* as a poetic form would appear to be a matter of style and presentation rather than of subject-matter and theme: it is short and rapid in exposition. Its frequent coincidence with the chivalric ethic seems to be largely fortuitous, though a vaguer 'romantic' quality is inherent, and the presence of the supernatural tends to be a distinguishing mark of the form.

Sir Degrevant

In this poem, we are reminded that the order of knighthood is not only an ideal, but a social reality. The hero is a knight-errant, but also a landlord, and though he seeks his adventures in remote and exotic parts of the world, his home is a solid English country estate. With a realistic social and economic context such as we find in this poem, it might be argued that the true chivalric romance is impossible. Indeed, it was asserted above that romance necessarily disengaged itself from such a context, and that it was this as much as anything that distinguished it from the heroic epic. Nevertheless, there was an irreducible element of idealism in the social institution of knighthood, however large the discrepancy between theory and practice. As Gervase Mathew expresses it:

'For a considerable section of the ruling classes, the slowly altering ideals of knighthood and of knightly conduct formed a standard of values, at times consciously followed, at times consciously sinned-against, but always pre-supposed.' (p. 354)

It is out of this situation that *Sir Degrevant* derives its status as a romance of chivalry. From this poem, as, though to a much greater degree, from *Sir Gawain and the Green Knight*, we obtain some insight into what it might have been like to be a knight. We see a recognizably human personality facing the problems and pressures of the chivalric ideal. The ideal is not explored in depth as in *Sir Gawain*, but it does supply a context which gives meaning and unity to the hero's experience. This is illustrated best in the first excerpt, but though the second is specifically chosen for its romance atmosphere, it also suggests the point. *Sir Degrevant* is formally attached to the Arthurian cycle, but it relies little on the glamour of that world. The setting, as Kane says, is one of 'English fields and deerparks and substantial country houses, full of

good food and drink and furnishings just a shade too rare and expensive'
(p. 90). The hero is summoned back from the Holy Land where he has been
undertaking deeds of arms for his own renown, by news of the trespasses of his
neighbour, the Earl, on his land. The Earl is 'unchivalrous' in every sense
relevant to the poem, for, to this poet, as to Chaucer, 'he is gentil that dooeth
gentil dedes'. It is Degrevant's behaviour when he arrives back in England
that establishes the particular flavour of the poem's chivalry, for the hero's
first action is to compensate his tenants and repair his fences. Further, he seeks
redress by law, in the first instance, not by force of arms. Only when his
attempts are spurned with contempt by his powerful neighbour does he resort
to violence. Then, of course, he reveals much more conventional heroic qualities. Yet even here, Degrevant's tactics are realistic. He lays an ambush for the
Earl, and opens hostilities with a flight of arrows. There is no formal combat
between the two adversaries, though this seems to be because the Earl shirks it.

The love-relationship between Degrevant and Myldore, the Earl's daughter,
described in the second passage, is not a particularly sophisticated one. The lady
is not distant or imperious—indeed, her initial greeting of the hero seems rather
naïvely enthusiastic—and her refusal to let him seduce her is made in terms of
everyday morality, even though her passion is, if anything, the stronger:

> 'Thou touchest non swych thing
> Or thou wed me with a ryng,
> And maryage fulfylle.' (IX. 526–8)

The function of this passage is, as L. F. Casson says in his edition, 'to fulfil the
same purpose as Acrasia's Bower of Bliss, or the description of Madeline's
chamber: to stupefy the hero's senses and make credible his attempted seduction
of Myldore'.[38] Yet there is a significant difference, for the fruits and 'lucent
syrops tinct with cinnamon' of *The Eve of Saint Agnes* are not there to be
eaten, but solely to create atmosphere, and the more homely delicacies here
obviously are consumed. The splendour here—architecture, furnishings and
food—is luxurious in terms of the actual life of the contemporary aristocracy
seen *couleur de rose*. The objects described are, on the whole, the best that could
be got for money at the time when the poem was written—the towels from
Aylsham, the glass from Westphalia, for example. There are more fabulous
details such as the curtain cords of mermaids' hair won by Duke Betyse, which
give a more exotic heightening to the scene, but on the whole the poet's
characteristically realistic vision prevails even here. It must be admitted, all the
same, that the atmospheric effect does not come off. The vision is too clear for
romantic sensual abandon. It would take a more perverse man than Degrevant
to be excited by the prospect of making love beneath the stony gaze of all

[38] L. F. Casson (ed.), *Sir Degrevant*, E.E.T.S., O.S. 221 (1944), p. lxxiv

those saints and evangelists in the roof, while a more insensitive one would not notice anyway. And this is just as well, for Degrevant is no hot Latin, but an English gentleman who is designed for marriage and a large family. It is fitting that our discussion of English medieval romance should close with so respectable an apotheosis.

NOTE TO THE TEXT

The following extracts are printed, with the minimum of emendation, from the manuscript generally accepted as the most authoritative for the particular text. Additions to the text are placed in square brackets. All abbreviations and contractions are silently expanded, and modern punctuation, capitalization and word-division are used throughout. In accordance with usual practice in *York Medieval Texts*, ȝ is replaced by *y*, *gh*, *w* or *s* as appropriate, and þ by *th* (þþ is also simplified to *th*); *u/v* and *i/j* are printed as vowel or consonant according to modern usage.

I. King Horn

THIS is the earliest extant ME romance, probably dating from the second quarter of the thirteenth century. It belongs to the so-called *Matter of England*, that is, romances which purport to deal with England before the Conquest. It may dimly reflect events which took place during the Viking raids on England, or may be of more exclusively Norse provenance. The story also survives in *Horn et Rimel*, a thirteenth-century Anglo-French poem, and in the fourteenth-century English romance *Horn Child*. None of these versions seem to be directly connected, though all may go back to a lost Old English narrative. However, the immediate source of King Horn is almost certainly a French poem. Three MSS survive: I print from the earliest.

MS: Cambridge University Library Gg.4.27.2
Dialect: Southern with South-eastern and Midland forms
Edition: King Horn, Floriz and Blauncheflur, etc., G. H. McKnight, E.E.T.S., O.S. 14 (1901)
Text: In forms of the past participle, the main stem and prefix i/y are printed without hyphenation, according to the manuscript practice.

(The king of Suddene is killed by pirates, and his son, Horn, captured. Horn is spared because of his beauty, but set adrift with his twelve companions. They come ashore in Westernesse, and are kindly received by King Aylmar, whose daughter, Rymenhild, falls in love with Horn, and persuades his friend Athulf to arrange a meeting with him.)

(399)   Horn in herte leide
        Al that he him seide.
        He yeode in wel righte
        To Rymenhild the brighte.
        On knes he him sette   5
        And sweteliche hure grette.
        Of his feire sighte
        Al the bur gan lighte.
        He spac faire speche;
        Ne dorte him noman teche.   10

8–9. A similar detail occurs in *Horn et Rimel*. Like the flame which issues from the sleeping Havelok's mouth, it may be taken as an indication of the hero's noble birth, but it is not a trait exclusive to romance.

'Wel thu sitte and softe,
Rymenhild the brighte,
With thine maidenes sixe
That the sitteth nixte.
Kinges stuard ure   15
Sende me in to bure.
With the speke Ihc scholde;
Seie me what thu woldest.
Seie, and Ich schal here,
What thi wille were.'   20
   Rymenhild up gan stonde
And tok him bi the honde.
Heo sette him on pelle,
Of wyn to drinke his fulle.
Heo makede him faire chere   25
And tok him abute the swere.
Ofte heo him custe,
So wel so hire luste.
'Horn,' heo sede, 'withute strif
Thu schalt have me to thi wif.   30
Horn, have of me rewthe,
And plist me thi trewthe.'
   Horn tho him bithoghte
What he speke mighte.
'Crist,' quath he, 'the wisse,   35
And yive the hevene blisse
Of thine husebonde,
Wher he beo in londe.
Ihc am ibore to lowe
Such wimman to knowe.   40
Ihc am icome of thralle,
And fundling bifalle.
Ne feolle hit the of cunde
To spuse beo me bunde.
Hit nere no fair wedding   45
Bitwexe a thral and a king.'

43-4. 'It would not become your birth to be bound to me as a wife.'

Tho gan Rymenhild mislyke,
And sore gan to sike.
Armes heo gan bughe;
Adun he feol iswoghe.   50
   Horn in herte was ful wo,
And tok hire on his armes two.
He gan hire for to kesse,
Wel ofte mid ywisse.
'Lemman,' he sede, 'dere,   55
Thin herte nu thu stere.
Help me to knighte,
Bi al thine mighte
To my lord the king,
That he me yive dubbing.   60
Thanne is mi thralhod
Iwent in to knighthod,
And I schal wexe more,
And do, lemman, thi lore.'
   Rymenhild, that swete thing,   65
Wakede of hire swoghning.
'Horn,' quath heo, 'wel sone
That schal beon idone.
Thu schalt beo dubbed knight
Are come seve night.   70
Have her this cuppe,
And this ring ther uppe,
To Aylbrus and stuard,
And se he holde foreward.
Seie Ich him biseche,   75
With loveliche speche,
That he adun falle

---

49. 'She let her arms fall' (from Horn's neck)
50. An indication of the emotionalism of the courtly romance.
70. 'before the week is out'
71-4. The text is corrupt, but the sense is clear enough: 'Take this cup, and this ring along with it, to Aylbrus the steward, and see that he keeps his promise.'

Bifore the king in halle,
And bidde the king arighte
Dubbe the to knighte.   80
With selver and with golde
Hit wurth him wel iyolde.
Crist him lene spede
Thin erende to bede.'
  Horn tok his leve,   85
For hit was negh eve.
Athelbrus he soghte
And yaf him that he broghte,
And tolde him ful yare
Hu he hadde ifare,   90
And sede him his nede,
And bihet him his mede.
  Athelbrus also swithe
Went to halle blive.
'Kyng,' he sede, 'thu leste   95
A tale mid the beste.
Thu schalt bere crune
Tomorewe in this tune.
Tomorewe is thi feste;
Ther bihoveth geste.   100
Hit nere noght forloren
For to knighti Child Horn,
Thin armes for to welde—
God knight he schal yelde.'
  The king sede sone,   105
'That is wel idone.
Horn me wel iquemeth;
God knight him bisemeth.
He schal have mi dubbing
And afterward mi derling.   110

---

82. 'He will be well rewarded for it.'
110. This detail occurs only in the Cambridge MS and is probably not
authentic, since it soon becomes clear that Avlmar has no intention of giving
his 'derling' Rymenhild to Horn.

And alle his feren twelf
He schal knighten himself.
Alle he schal hem knighte
Bifore me this nighte.'
Til the light of day sprang   115
Ailmar him thughte lang.
The day bigan to springe,
Horn com bivore the kinge,
Mid his twelf ifere;
Sume hi were luthere.   120
Horn he dubbede to knighte
With swerd and spures brighte.
He sette him on a stede whit;
Ther nas no knight hym ilik.
He smot him a litel wight   125
And bed him beon a god knight.
    Athulf fel a knes thar
Bivore the kyng Aylmar.
'King,' he sede, 'so kene,
Grante me a bene.   130
Nu is knight Sire Horn
That in Suddene was iboren.
Lord he is of londe,
Over us that bi him stonde.
Thin armes he hath, and scheld,   135
To fighte with upon the feld.
Let him us alle knighte,
For that is ure righte.'
    Aylmar sede sone ywis,
'Do nu that thi wille is.'   140
Horn adun lighte
And makede hem alle knightes.
Murie was the feste,
Al of faire gestes,

131. knight: MS knigh

120. *luthere*, 'hateful', *i.e.* the traitor Fykenhild.

Ac Rymenhild nas noght ther, 145
And that hire thughte seve yer.
After Horn heo sente,
And he to bure wente.
Nolde he noght go one—
Athulf was his mone. 150
Rymenhild on flore stod,
Hornes come hire thughte god,
And sede, 'Welcome, Sire Horn,
And Athulf, knight the biforn.
Knight, nu is thi time 155
For to sitte bi me.
Do nu that thu er of spake,
To thi wif thu me take.
Ef thu art trewe of dedes,
Do nu ase thu sedes. 160
Nu thu hast wille thine,
Unbind me of my pine.'
   'Rymenhild,' quath he, 'beo stille;
Ihc wulle don al thi wille.
Also hit mot bitide, 165
Mid spere I schal furst ride,
And mi knighthod prove,
Ar Ihc the ginne to wowe.
We beth knightes yonge,
Of o dai al isprunge, 170
And of ure mestere
So is the manere,
With sume othere knighte
Wel for his lemman fighte,
Or he eni wif take; 175

145–6. 'But Rymenhild was not there: the time seemed like seven years to her.'

165–82. This is an example of the classic motivation of chivalric romance. Note also the implied concept of knighthood as a way of life.

171–6. 'And such is the custom of our profession: for a knight to fight for his mistress against another knight before he takes a wife: therefore it behoves me to make (more) haste.'

Forthi me stondeth the more rape.
Today, so Crist me blesse,
Ihc wulle do pruesse
For thi luve in the felde,
Mid spere and mid schelde.   180
If Ihc come to lyve,
Ihc schal the take to wyve.'
    'Knight,' quath heo, 'trewe,
Ihc wene Ihc mai the leve.
Tak nu her this gold ring,   185
God him is the dubbing.
There is upon the ringe
Igrave, 'Rymenhild the yonge'.
Ther nis non betere an onder sunne,
That eni man of telle cunne.   190
For my luve thu hit were,
And on thi finger thu him bere.
The stones beoth of suche grace,
That thu ne schalt in none place
Of none duntes beon ofdrad,   195
Ne on bataille beon amad,
Ef thu loke theran
And thenke upon thi lemman.
    And Sir Athulf, thi brother,
He schal have another.   200
Horn, Ihc the biseche
With loveliche speche,
Crist yeve god erndinge,
The ayen to bringe.'

(Horn soon finds adventures, and destroys a band of paynims, but the traitor
Fykenhild betrays the love of Horn and Rymenhild to the king, and the hero
is banished. He takes service with the King of Ireland, killing a Saracen giant
for him. The king offers him his daughter in marriage, but Horn remains
faithful to Rymenhild. At the end of seven years, he receives word that
Rymenhild is being compelled to marry another prince. He returns to Westernesse, and arrives at the wedding-feast disguised as a palmer.)

(1141)   Horn tok burdon and scrippe,   205

And wrong his lippe.
He makede him a ful chere,
And al bicolmede his swere.
He makede him unbicomelich
Hes he nas nevremore ilich.   210
   He com to the gateward,
That him answerede hard.
Horn bad undo softe
Mani tyme and ofte.
Ne mighte he awynne   215
That he come therinne.
Horn gan to the gate turne,
And that wiket unspurne.
The boye hit scholde abugge;
Horn threu him over the brigge,   220
That his ribbes him tobrake,
And suthe com in atte gate.
He sette him wel lowe,
In beggeres rowe.
He lokede him abute,   225
With his colmie snute.
He segh Rymenhild sitte
Ase heo were of witte,
Sore wepinge and yerne;
Ne mighte hure noman wurne.   230
He lokede in eche halke;
Ne segh he nowhar walke
Athulf his felawe,
That he cuthe knowe.
Athulf was in the ture   235
Abute for to pure
After his comynge,
Yef schup him wolde bringe.

---

206. 'and contorted his features'
209–10. 'He made himself repulsive, such as he never was in his life.'
223–4. It was the custom in the early Middle Ages to admit a few beggars to the wedding-feast, and the bride herself served them (249ff.).

He segh the se flowe,
And Horn nowar rowe.   240
He sede upon his songe,
'Horn, nu thu ert wel longe.
Rymenhild thu me toke
That I scholde loke:
Ihc habbe kept hure evre—   245
Com nu other nevre.
I ne may no leng hure kepe;
For sorewe nu Y wepe.'
   Rymenhild ros of benche,
Wyn for to schenche,   250
After mete in sale,
Bothe wyn and ale.
On horn he bar an honde,
So lawe was in londe.
Knightes and squier   255
Alle dronken of the ber,
Bute Horn al one
Nadde thereof no mone.
Horn sat upon the grunde;
Him thughte he was ibunde.   260
He sede, 'Quen so hende,
To meward thu wende.
Thu yef us with the furste;
The beggeres beoth ofthurste.'
Hure horn heo leide adun,   265
And fulde him of a brun,
His bolle of a galun,
For heo wende he were a glotoun.

243-4. 'You entrusted Rymenhild to my care.'

254. *lawe*—the sense here is 'custom'.

260. 'It seemed to him that he was overpowered (by his emotions).'

263. *with the furste*: either 'along with those you serve first' or 'along with those who are first (highest) in rank'.

266. *a brun*. The distinction is being made between the vessel suitable for the aristocracy and that for the beggars: most medieval pottery was brown, but the drinking-horn would naturally be white.

He seide, 'Have this cuppe,
And this thing ther uppe.   270
Ne saw Ihc nevre, so Ihc wene,
Beggere that were so kene.'
Horn tok hit his ifere,
And sede, 'Quen so dere,
Wyn nelle Ihc, muche ne lite,   275
Bute of cuppe white.
Thu wenest I beo a beggere,
And Ihc am a fissere,
Wel feor icome bi este,
For fissen at thi feste.   280
Mi net lith her bi honde,
Bi a wel fair stronde.
Hit hath ileie there
Fulle seve yere.
Ihc am icome to loke   285
Ef eni fiss hit toke.
Ihc am icome to fisse;
Drink to me of disse.
Drink to Horn of horne,
Feor Ihc am i-orne.'   290
Rymenhild him gan bihelde;
Hire heorte bigan to chelde.
Ne kneu heo noght his fissing,
Ne Horn hymselve nothing;
Ac wunder hire gan thinke   295
Whi he had to Horn drinke.
Heo fulde hire horn with wyn,

---

270. *thing*: perhaps a scribe's error for *ring*.

271ff. Horn's refusal of the bowl and insistence on the drinking-horn of wine is probably intended to hint his rank to Rymenhild.

273. 'Horn handed it to his companions'

281. Earlier in the poem, Rymenhild's love for Horn has been likened to a net. Probably here the net signifies Horn's love. If the application is still to Rymenhild, then Horn is suggesting that he has come to see whether anyone has replaced him in her affections—'My net has lain here on a fair shore for seven years: now I have come to see if it has caught a fish.'

293. 'She recognized neither (the allusion to) fishing, nor Horn himself'

And dronk to the pilegrym.
Heo sede, 'Drink thi fulle,
And suthe thu me telle   300
If thu evre isighe
Horn under wude lighe.'
Horn dronk of horn a stunde,
And threu the ring to grunde.
The quen yede to bure,   305
With hire maidenes foure.
Tho fond heo what heo wolde—
A ring igraven of golde,
That Horn of hure hadde.
Sore hure dradde   310
That Horn isterve were,
For the ring was there.
Tho sente heo a damisele
After the palmere.
'Palmere,' quath heo, 'trewe,   315
The ring that thu threwe,
Thu seie whar thu hit nome,
And whi thu hider come."
He sede, 'Bi Seint Gile,
Ihc habbe go mani mile,   320
Wel feor biyonde weste,
To seche my beste.
I fond Horn Child stonde,
To schupward in londe.
He sede he wolde agesse   325
To arive in Westernesse.
The schip nam to the flode,
With me and Horn the gode.

---

302. *under wude lighe*: a common formula .. 'under the wood-groves', *i.e.*
'anywhere in the world'.

304. *to grunde*, 'to the bottom' (of the horn)

319. *Seint Gile*: the abbey of St Gilles, near Nîmes in Provence, was a famous
medieval place of pilgrimage.

323-4. *stonde to schupward*, 'standing near the ship', *i.e.* 'about to embark'

327. *nam to the flode*, 'put out to sea'

Horn was sik and deide,
And faire he me preide: 330
"Go with the ringe
To Rymenhild the yonge."
Ofte he hit custe,
God yeve his saule reste.'
   Rymenhild sede at the furste,   335
'Herte, nu thu berste,
For Horn nastu namore,
That the hath pined the so sore.'
Heo feol on hire bedde
Ther heo knif hudde,   340
To sle with king lothe,
And hure selve bothe,
In that ulke nighte,
If Horn come ne mighte.
Ac Horn anon hire kepte.   345
He wipede that blake of his swere,
And sede, "Quen so swete and dere,
Ihc am Horn thin owe;
Ne canstu me noght knowe?
Ihc am Horn of Westernesse—   350
In armes thu me cusse.'
Hi custe hem mid ywisse,
And makeden muche blisse.

(Horn kills his rival and sets out to regain his own kingdom, where he finds his mother, who has been living in hiding. The plot then repeats itself: Rymenhild is about to be forced into yet another unwelcome marriage when Horn returns, disguised as a harper, rescues her, and is finally married.)

340-4. 'where she had (hidden) a knife, with which to slay the hateful king and herself that very night, if Horn should not come'

345. 'but Horn prevented her.' There appears to be a line missing here, though there is no gap in the MS.

II. Havelok

SLIGHTLY later than *King Horn*, but apparently in existence before 1300, this poem also belongs to the *Matter of England* and seems to reflect the political union of England and Denmark in the eleventh century. One or two of the names are historical, but the plot is a familiar one in folk-tale, and the historical element must be very slight. The earliest version of the story is in the twelfth-century Anglo-Norman chronicle of Gaimar, *Lestoire des Engleis*, and it also survives in the form of a Breton *lai* of the same period. An English version, related to both of these, is interpolated into one of the MSS of the fourteenth-century English chronicle of Robert Mannyng of Brunne. *Havelok*, however, seems to derive from a quite distinct version of the material. A French original is likely, but the treatment is very free. The story is localized in Lincolnshire in all surviving versions: Grim, the hero's foster-father, is the eponymous founder of Grimsby, and the town seal bears witness to the connexion.

I print from the only complete MS, but fragments are preserved in some scraps of MS in the University Library, Cambridge.

MS: Bodleian, Laud Misc. 108

Dialect: East Midland, of North Lincs.

Editions: The Lay of Havelok the Dane, ed. W. W. Skeat, 2nd edn. revised K. Sisam (Oxford, 1915): also in W. H. French and C. B. Hale, *Middle English Metrical Romances* (New York, 1930)

Text: The spelling practices of the scribe are curious, and the usual ME spelling has been restored in a number of instances. The scribe uses th for -ht, and sometimes for -t. Such spellings are silently modernized, as are the following, which occur frequently: *with* (MS *wit*), *and* (MS *an*), *hu* (MS *hw*), *mikel* (MS *mike*).

(On his death, Athelwold, the king of England, leaves his daughter in the care of Godrich, Earl of Cornwall. He is to marry her to the fairest and strongest man in the kingdom, and then hand the government of the country to her. However, Godrich usurps power and has Goldboru imprisoned. Meanwhile, a similar situation is developing in Denmark, where Earl Godard is made guardian of Havelok, the king's son, and his two sisters. He seizes the kingdom, kills the girls, and commands the fisherman, Grim, to drown the boy. Grim and his wife, however, recognize Havelok's royal birth when they see a flame issuing from the sleeping child's mouth. They flee with him to England, and bring him up as one of their own children.)

54

(749)   Grim was fishere swithe god,
       And mikel couthe on the flod;
       Mani god fish therinne he tok,
       Bothe with net and with hok.
       He tok the sturgiun and the qual,   5
       And the turbut and lax withal;
       He tok the sele and the hwel—
       He spedde ofte swithe wel.
       Keling he tok, and tumberel,
       Hering and the makerel,   10
       The butte, the schulle, the thornebake.
       Gode paniers dede he make
       On til him, and other thrinne
       Til hise sones, to beren fish inne,
       Up o londe to selle and fonge.   15
       Forbar he neyther tun ne gronge
       That he ne to-yede with his ware;
       Kam he nevere hom hand-bare,
       That he ne broucte bred and sowel
       In his shirte, or in his couel,   20
       In his poke, benes and korn—
       His swink ne havede he nowt forlorn.
       And hwan he tok the grete laumprei,
       Ful wel he couthe the rihte wei
       To Lincolne, the gode boru.   25

4. net: MS neth. These and similar spellings are henceforth silently emended.
16. neyther: MS neythe

---

4. The MS spelling *neth* and the others like it probably indicate the work of a scribe of Norman birth who found difficulty in reproducing the English vernacular.

7–10. Whale, seal, sturgeon and porpoise all regularly appear in medieval accounts of feasts, with what accuracy one cannot say. However, in this list, the conventional items may be mixed with some first-hand knowledge of a fisherman's business.

23. 'A "great" lamprey could weigh as much as five pounds, and sold for 3/-' (French and Hale). It was a prized delicacy, as the legendary account of Henry I's death of a surfeit of lampreys testifies.

Ofte he yede it thoru and thoru,
Til he havede al wel sold,
And therefore the penies told.
Thanne he com thenne, he were blithe,
For hom he brouhte fele sithe   30
Wastels, simenels with the horn,
Hise pokes fulle of mele and korn,
Netes flesh, shepes and swines,
And hemp to maken of gode lines,
And stronge ropes to hise netes: 35
In the se weren he ofte setes.

Thusgate Grim him fayre ledde:
Him and his genge wel he fedde
Wel twelf winter, other more.
Havelok was war that Grim swank sore   40
For his mete, and he lay at hom:
Thouhte, 'Ich am nou no grom,
Ich am wel waxen, and wel may eten
More than evere Grim may geten.
Ich ete more, bi God on live,   45
Than Grim and hise children five!
It ne may nouht ben thus longe,
Goddot! Y wile with them gange
For to leren sum god to gete;
Swinken Ich wolde for mi mete.   50
It is no schame forto swinken—

27. al: MS wol
48. them: MS the

---

31. Wastels and simenels were both cakes of fine flour: the simenel was twisted so as to look like a horn.

36. Corrupt: the meaning is perhaps: 'They (the nets) were often set in the sea'.

40. *Havelok*. The name is an Anglicized form of the Irish *Abloc*, which was often substituted for the ON *Olafr*. The hero may be identified with the famous tenth-century Viking, Olafr Cuaran. The nickname *Cuaran*, which means 'rawhide sandal' in Irish, is given to Havelok in the Anglo-French versions.

The man that may wel eten and drinken
That nouht ne have but on swink long;
To liggen at hom it is ful strong.
God yelde him ther I ne may,   55
That haveth me fed to this day!
Gladlike I wile the paniers bere;
Ich wot, ne shal it me nouht dere,
They ther be inne a birthene gret
Al so hevi als a net.   60
Shal Ich nevere lengere dwelle,
Tomorwen shal Ich forth pelle.'

On the morwen, hwan it was day,
He stirt up sone and nought ne lay,
And cast a panier on his bac   65
With fish givéled also a stac;
Also michel he bar him one
So he foure, bi mi mone!
Wel he it bar, and solde it wel,
The silver he brouhte hom ilk del;   70
Al that he ther-fore tok,
Withheld he nouht a ferthinges nok.
So yede he forth ilke day,
That he nevere at home lay,
So wolde he his mestere lere.   75
Bifel it so a strong dere
Bigan to rise of korn of bred,
That Grim ne couthe no god red,

70. ilk: MS il

52–3. *nouht .. ne ouht*, 'ought not', thus: 'The man who can drink and eat
heartily ought not to have that (*i.e.* food and drink) without long toil' (French
and Hale).

60. *net* (MS *neth*) derives from OE *nēat*, 'an ox', as the rhyme indicates.

67–8. 'He alone bore as much as the four of them (Grim and his three sons)
in my opinion.'

72. Nearly all coins were silver: for small change, pennies would be cut into
halves and quarters (French and Hale).

73–86. Compare this with *King Horn* 165–82.

C

Hu he sholde his meiné fede.
Of Havelok havede he michel drede,   80
For he was stronge and wel mouhte ete
More thanne hevere mouhte he gete;
Ne he ne mouhte on the se take
Neyther lenge ne thornbake,
Ne non other fish that douhte   85
His meyné feden with he mouhte.
Of Havelok he havede kare,
Hwilgat that he mihte fare.

Of his children was him nouht,
On Havelok was al hise thouht,   90
And seyde, 'Havelok, dere sone,
I wene that we deye mone
For hunger, this dere is so strong,
And hure mete is uten long.
Betere is that thu henne gonge   95
Than thu here dwelle longe;
Hethen thou mayt gangen to late.
Thou canst ful wel the rihte gate
To Lincolne, the gode borw,
Thou havest it gon ful oft thoru.   100
Of me ne is me nouht a slo,
Betere is that thu thider go,
For there is mani god man inne,
There thou mayt thi mete winne.
But wo is me! thou art so naked,   105
Of mi seyl Y wolde the were maked
A cloth, thou mihtest inne gongen,
Sone, no cold that thu ne fonge.'

88. mihte: MS micthe

85–6. 'nor any other fish which were of use, with (which) he might feed his household'
89. 'He did not think of his children's welfare'
94. *uten long*, 'long out', *i.e.* exhausted
101. 'I am not worth a sloe-berry'

He tok the sheres of the nayl,
And made him a couel of the sayl,   110
And Havelok dide it sone on.
Havede neyther hosen ne shon,
Ne none kines other wede;
To Lincolne barefot he yede.
Hwan he kam ther, he was ful wil,   115
Navede he no frend to gangen til;
Two dayes ther fastinde he yede,
That non for his werk wolde him fede;
The thridde day herde he calle:
'Bermen, bermen, hider forth alle!'   120
Sprongen forth so sparke on glede.
Havelok shof dun nyne or ten
Riht amidewarde the fen,
And stirte forth to the kok,
That he bouhte at the brigge.   125
The bermen let he alle ligge,
And bar the mete to the castel
And gat him there a ferthing wastel.

Thet other day kepte he the ok
Swithe yerne the erles kok,   130
Til that he say him on the brigge,
And bi him mani fishes ligge.
The erles mete havede he bouht

109. sheres: MS shres
113. other: MS othe
131. brigge: MS bigge
133. erles: MS herles

---

115. *he was ful wil,* 'he was quite at a loss'
120. A line appears to be missing before line 121.
124. A line appears to be missing before line 125.
125. The bridge spanned the Witham. Lincoln castle is about half a mile away, up a steep hill.
129-30. 'The next day also, he kept a sharp look-out for the Earl's cook'
133-4. Note the construction: 'the Earl's meat of Cornwall'.

Of Cornwalie, and kalde oft:
'Bermen, bermen, hider swithe!'   135
Havelok it herde and was ful blithe
That he herde 'Bermen' calle.
Alle made he hem dune falle
That in his gate yeden and stode—
Wel sixtene laddes gode.   140
Als he lep the kok til,
He shof hem alle upon an hyl,
Astirte til him with his rippe,
And bigan the fish to kippe.
He bar up wel a carte-lode   145
Of segges, laxes, of playces brode,
Of grete laumprees, and of eles;
Sparede he neyther tos ne heles
Til that he to the castel cam,
That men from him his birthene nam.   150
Than men haveden holpen him doun
With the birthene of his croun,
The kok stod and on him low,
And thouhte him stalworthe man ynow,
And seyde, 'Wiltu ben with me?   155
Gladlike wile Ich feden the;
Wel is set the mete thu etes,
And the hire that thu getes.'

'Goddot!' quoth he, 'leve sire,
Bidde Ich you non other hire,   160
But yeveth me inow to ete,
Fir and water Y wile you fete,
The fir blowe, and ful well maken;
Stickes kan Ich breken and kraken,

159. Goddot: MS Soddot

---

148. *i.e.* 'he hurried'.
157-8. 'Your board and wages will be generous.'
159-70. The list of the hero's accomplishments is a common feature of romance: these, however, are remarkably homely, cf. IX. 33ff.

And kindlen ful wel a fir,   165
And maken it to brennen shir;
Ful wel kan Ich cleven shides,
Eles to-turven of here hides;
Ful wel kan Ich dishes swilen,
And don al that the evere wilen.'   170
Quoth the kok, 'Wile I no more;
Go thu yunder and sit thore,
And Y shal yeve the ful fair bred,
And make the broys in the led.
Sit now doun and et ful yerne: 175
Datheit hwo the mete werne!'

Havelok sette him dun anon,
Also stille als a ston,
Til he havede ful wel eten.
Tho havede Havelok fayre geten.   180
Hwan he havede eten inow,
He kam to the welle, water up-drowe,
And filde ther a michel so;
Bad he non ageyn him go,
But bitwen his hondes he bar it in,   185
Al him one he to the kichin.
Bad he non him water to fete,
Ne fro brigge to bere the mete.
He bar the turves, he bar the star,
The wode fro the brigge he bar;   190
Al that evere shulden he nytte,
Al he drow and al he citte;
Wolde he never haven rest,
More than he were a best.

183. ther: MS the
186. Al: MS A
188. brigge: MS bigge

---

168. *i.e.* 'skin eels'.
176. 'A curse on the man who refuses you food!'
184. 'He didn't ask anyone to go and meet him' (*i.e.* to help him with the pail)

Of alle men was he mest meke,   195
Lauhwinde ay and blithe of speke;
Evere he was glad and blithe,
His sorwe he couthe ful wel mithe.
It ne was non so litel knave,
For leyken ne for to plawe,   200
That he ne wode with him pleye:
The children that yeden in the weie
Of him, he deden al here wille,
And with him leykeden here fille.

Him loveden alle, stille and bolde,   205
Knihtes, children, yunge and holde;
Alle him loveden that him sowen,
Bothen heye men and lowe.
Of him ful wide the word sprong,
Hu he was mikel, hu he was strong,   210
Hu fayr man God him havede maked,
Buton that he was almest naked;
For he ne havede nouht to shride
But a kouel ful unride,
That ful [was] and swithe wicke—   215
Was it nouht worth a fir-sticke.
The cok bigan of him to rewe,
And bouhte him clothes al spannewe;
He bouhte him bothe hosen and shon,
And sone did him dones on.   220
Hwan he was clothed, osed and shod,
Was non so fayr under God

202. yeden: MS yden
203. here: MS he
206. knihtes: MS knictes

195ff. Havelok has the usual qualities of the popular hero of folk-tale. Most of them would also be appropriate to the hero of chivalric romance, but they are illustrated here, on the whole, in non-chivalric circumstances.

199–201. 'There was no boy so little for (the purposes of) sporting and playing that Havelok would not play with him'

220. 'and soon made him put them on'

That evere moder bere.
It was nevere man that yemede   225
In kinneriche, that so wel semede
King or cayser forto be,
Than he was shrid, so semede he;
For thanne he weren alle samen
At Lincolne, at the gamen,   230
And the erles men woren alle thore,
Than was Havelok bi the shuldren more
Than the meste that ther kam.
In armes him noman nam
That he doune sone ne caste.   235
Havelok stod over hem als a mast.
Als he was heie, al he was long,
He was bothe stark and strong.
In Engelond non hise per
Of strengthe that evere kam him ner.   240
Als he was strong, so was he softe;
They a man him misdede ofte,
Nevere more he him misdede,
Ne hond on him with yvele leyde.
Of bodi was he mayden clene;   245
Nevere yete in game ne in grene
With hire ne wolde leyke ne lye
No more than it were a strie.
In that time al Hengelond
Therl Godrich havede in his hond,   250
And he gart komen into the tun
Mani erl and mani barun;
And alle that lives were
In Englond thanne wer there
That they haveden after sente   255

234–5. 'There was nobody who grappled with him who wasn't soon thrown down.'

247. Either corrupt, or a line missing here. Kölbing emended *hire* to *hore*, thus: 'He would neither sport nor lie with a whore, any more than if she were an old hag.'

To ben ther at the parlement.
With hem com mani champioun,
Mani wiht ladde, blac and brown,
And fel it so that yunge men,
Wel abouten nine or ten,   260
Bigunnen there for to layke.
Thider komen both stronge and wayke,
Thider komen lesse and more,
That in the borw thanne weren thore;
Chaunpiouns and stark laddes,   265
Bondemen with here gaddes,
Als he comen fro the plow;
Ther was sembling inow!
For it ne was non horse-knave,
Tho thei sholden in honde have,   270
That he ne kam thider the leyk to se.
Biforn here fet thanne lay a tre,
And putten with a mikel ston
The starke laddes, ful god won.
The ston was mikel and ek gret,   275
And al so hevi so a net;
Grund-stalwurthe man he sholde be
That mouhte liften it to his kne.
Was ther neyther clerc ne prest

257. champioun: MS chabioun
261. there: MS the
273. putten: MS pulten
277. stalwurthe: MS stalwrthe

---

256. A number of parliaments were, in fact, held at Lincoln, the earliest recorded being in 1213.

258. *blac and brown:* a characteristic tag. It may mean 'everyone', but more probably black and brown complexions distinguish the peasantry from the red and white of the nobility, and 'lad' in this poem tends to have a derogatory sense.

269-71. 'For there was no horse-boy, whatever work there might be on hand, who did not come there to see the sports.'

273. This sport was especially popular among the Germanic peoples: however, heroes of romance are often proficient in it.

That mihte liften it to his brest.   280
Therwith putten the chaunpiouns
That thider comen with the barouns.
Hwo-so mihte putten thore
Biforn another an inch or more,
Wore he yung, wore he hold,   285
He was for a kempe told.
Also thei stoden and often stareden,
The chaunpiouns, and ek the ladden,
And he made mikel strout
Abouten the altherbeste but.   290
Havelok stod, and lokede theretil,
And of puttingge he was ful wil,
For nevere yete ne saw he or
Putten the ston, or thanne thore.
Hise mayster bad him gon therto,   295
Als he couthe therwith do.
Tho hise mayster it him bad,
He was of him sore adrad;
Thereto he stirte sone anon,
And kipte up that hevi ston,   300
That he sholde puten withe.
He putte, at the firste sithe,
Over alle that ther wore,
Twelve fote and sumdel more.
The chaunpiouns that put sowen,   305
Shuldreden he ilc other and lowen:
Wolden he no more to putting gange,

287. thei: MS the
304. twelve: MS twel

---

286. *kempe:* the word seems to denote the champion athlete, while the
chaunpioun is merely the competent performer.
287. *stareden:* though a feeble rhyme, this makes sense. However, Sisam's
emendation *stadden* (*pp.* of ON *stethja*, 'looked on') is attractive, and considering
the strong ON element in the poem's vocabulary, quite likely.
292. 'and he was quite ignorant of (the art of) putting'
296. 'to do as well as he could with it'
306. 'they nudged one another and laughed'
C*

But seyde, 'We dwellen her to longe!'
This selkouth mihte nouht ben hyd,
Ful sone it was ful loude kid   310
Of Havelok, hu he warp the ston
Over the laddes everilkon;
Hu he was fayr, hu he was long,
Hu he was wiht, hu he was strong.
Thoruth England yede the speche   315
Hu he was strong and ek meke;
In the castle, up in the halle
The knihtes speken therof alle,
So that Godrich it herde wel
Ther speken of Havelok, everi del,   320
Hu he was strong man and hey,
Hu he was strong, and ek fri,
And thouhte Godrich, 'Thoru this knave
Shal Ich Engelond al have,
And mi sone after me,   325
For so I wile that it be.
The king, Athelwald, me dide swere
Upon al the messe-gere
That I shude his douhter yeve
The hexte that mihte live,   330
The beste, the fairest, the strangest ok;
That garte he me sweren on the bok.
Hwere mihte I finden ani so hey
So Havelok is, or so sley?
Thou Y souhte hethen into Ynde,   335
So fayr, so strong ne mihte Y finde.
Havelok is that ilke knave
That shal Goldeborw have.'

308. we: MS the
323. thouhte: MS thouthte

333–4. Godrich plays on the two senses of 'high': Havelok is the tallest man
in the land, and Godrich has promised to marry Goldeborw to the man of
noblest birth. But there is a further irony, since Havelok, the rightful king of
Denmark, is the 'highest' in that sense also.

335. *Ynde:* India is commonly used to suggest great distance and remoteness.

This thouhte [he] with trechery,
With traysoun and with felony,   340
For he wende that Havelok wore
Sum cherles sone, and no more;
Ne shulde he haven of Engellond
Onlepi forw in his hond
With hire that was thereof eyr,   345
That bothe was god and swithe fair.
He wende that Havelok wer a thral,
Ther-thoru he wende haven al
In Engelond, that hire riht was.
He was werse than Sathanas   350
That Jesu Crist in erthe shop:
Hanged worthe he on an hok!

(The marriage takes place, in spite of reluctance on both sides, and Havelok
takes Goldeboru back to Grimsby. At night, she sees the light from Havelok's
mouth, and a 'king-mark' on his shoulder. She is informed by an angel of his
birth and fortune, while Havelok also has a prophetic dream of greatness to
come. They sail for Denmark, accompanied by the three sons of Grim, and
are befriended there by Earl Ubbe.)

(1714) Hwan it was comen time to ete,
Hise wif dede Ubbe sone in fete,
And til hire seyde, al on gamen: 355
'Dame, thou and Havelok shulen ete samen,
And Goldeboru shal ete with me,
That is so fayr so flour on tre;
In al Denemark nis wimman
So fayr so sche, bi seint Johan!'   360
Thanne were set, and bord leyd,
And the beneysun was seyd,
Biforn hem com the beste mete
That king or cayser wolde ete:

359. nis wimman: MS is wimman

343–5. 'He should not have possession of a single furrow of English land
along with her who was the rightful heir to it'
363–8. A fairly typical romance banquet, though many are described at
much greater length.

Kranes, swannes, veneysun,   365
Lax, lampreys, and god sturgiun,
Pyment to drinke, and god claré,
Wyn hwit and red, ful god plenté.
Was therinne no page so lite
That evere wolde ale bite.   370
Of the mete forto telle,
Ne of the metes bidde I nouht dwelle:
That is the story for to lenge,
It wolde anuye this fayre genge.
But hwan he haveden the ilk thing deled,   375
And fele sithes haveden wosseyled,
And with gode drinkes seten longe,
And it was time for to gonge,
Ilk man to other he cam fro,
Thouhte Ubbe, 'Yf I late hem go,   380
Thus one foure, withouten mo,
So mote Ich brouke finger or to,
For this wimman bes mikel wo!
For hire shal men hire louerd slo."
He tok sone knihtes ten,   385
And wel sixti other men
With gode bowes and with gleives,
And sende him unto the greyves,

366. sturgiun: MS sturgun
372. nouht: MS nout
375. the ilk thing: MS the kilthing
379. Ilk: MS Il

369–70. *i.e.* everyone had expensive wine to drink: ale was the common drink of the country.

371–4. A common minstrel's formula: note the direct address to a listening audience.

376. *wosseyled:* i.e. drank healths in the manner of the Germanic peoples.

379–84. Such passages, rhyming on the same vowel, are quite common in *Havelok* and may be consciously imitated from the French assonant *tirades* common in the *chansons de geste*.

387. *gleives:* i.e. spears with a cutting hook near the end (French and Hale).

388. *greyve:* the word appears to derive from ON *greifi*, but the office probably corresponds to the OE *gerēfa*, the chief magistrate of a town or district.

The beste man of al the toun,
That was named Bernard Brun, 390
And bad him als he lovede his lif,
Havelok wel yemen and his wif,
And wel do wayten al the niht
Til the other day, that it were liht.
Bernard was trewe and swithe wiht, 395
In al the borw ne was no kniht
That betere couthe on stede riden,
Helm on heved, ne swerd bi side.
Havelok he gladlike understod,
With mikel love and herte god, 400
And did greythe a super riche,
Also he was no wiht chinche,
To his behove everilk dele,
That he mihte supe swithe wel.
Also he seten and sholde soupe, 405
So comes a ladde in a joupe
And with him sixti other stronge,
With swerdes drawen and knives longe,
Ilkan in hande a ful god gleive,
And seyde, 'Undo, Bernard the greyve! 410
Undo swithe and lat us in,
Or thu art ded, bi Seint Austin!'
Bernard stirt up, that was ful big,
And caste a brinie upon his rig,
And grop an ar, that was ful god, 415
Lep to the dore so he wore wod,
And seyde, 'Hwat are ye that are ther-oute,
That thus biginnen forto stroute?

392. yemen: MS ymen
403. everilk: MS everil

405ff. In spite of Ubbe's fears (383–4) the motive for the raid on Bernard's
house appears to be robbery. In the French poems, the outlaws want to carry
off Goldeboru, and this is clearly a better motivation.

415. *ar:* apparently 'oar' (OE *ār*) An oar is used as a weapon later in this
passage, by one of the sons of Grim, but here it may well be a scribal error for
ax.

Goth henne swithe, fule theves,
For, bi the Louerd that man on leves,   420
Shol Ich casten the dore open,
Summe of you shal Ich drepen!
And the othre shal Ich kesten
In feteres, and ful faste festen.'
'Hwat, have ye seid?' quoth a ladde.   425
'Wenestu that we ben adradde?
We shole at this dore gonge
Maugre thin, carl, or ouht longe.'
He gripen sone a bulder-ston
And let it fleye, ful god won,   430
Agen the dore, that it to-rof.
Avelok it saw and thider drof,
And the barre sone ut-drow,
That was unride and gret ynow,
And caste the dore open wide   435
And seide, 'Her shal Y now abide:
Comes swithe unto me:
Datheyt hwo you henne fle!'
'No,' quod on, 'that shaltou coupe,'
And bigan til him to loupe,   440
In his hand his swerd ut-drawe;
Havelok he wende thore have slawe.
And with [him] comen other two,
That him wolde of live have do.
Havelok lifte up the dore-tre,   445

437. me: MS me datheit
439. quod: MS quodh

421–2. 'If I open this door, I shall kill some of you!'
428–30. The house seems to be a wooden structure: again, perhaps, a pointer to the English antecedents of the story (French and Hale).
438. *you* is object: 'Cursed be the man who flees from you!'
445. The account of the combat is much less circumstantial in the French *Lai d'Havelok*, and more in keeping with an aristocratic mode. There, Havelok's weapon is an axe, the foster-brothers' share in the action is not specified and Havelok retreats to a monastery, where he defends himself by throwing down a huge stone on his enemies.

And at a dint he slow hem thre;
Was non of hem that his hernes
Ne lay ther-ute ageyn the sternes.
The ferthe that he sithen mette,
With the barre so he him grette   450
Bifor the heved, that the riht eye
Ut of the hole made he fleye,
And sithe clapte him on the crune
So that he stan-ded fel thor dune.
The fifte that he overtok   455
Gaf he a ful sor dint ok
Bitwen the sholdres ther he stod,
That he speu his herte blod.
The sixte wende for to fle,
And he clapte him with the tre   460
Riht in the fule necke so
That he smot hise necke on to.
Thanne the sixe weren doun feld,
The seventhe brayd ut his swerd,
And wolde Havelok riht in the eye.   465
And Havelok let the barre fleye,
And smot him sone ageyn the brest,
That havede he nevere schrifte of prest;
For he was ded on lesse hwile
Than men mouhte renne a mile.   470
Alle the othere weren ful kene:
A red thei taken hem bitwene
That he sholde him bihalve,
And brisen so that with no salve
Ne sholde him helen leche non.   475
They drowen ut swerdes, ful god won,

466. let the: MS le
468. schrifte: MS schifte

---

458. *speu*, 'vomited'. This is clearly the MS reading, but earlier editors read *spen* and emended to *spende*, 'spent'.

463–4. A bad rhyme: a line with *scheld* for *swerd* would mend it, and may have been in the original.

472–3. 'They made a plan between them to surround him'

And shoten on him so don on bere
Dogges that wolden him to-tere
Thanne men doth the bere beyte.
The laddes were kaske and teyte,   480
And umbiyeden him ilkon.
Sum smot with tre, and sum with ston;
Sum putten with gleyve in bac and side
And yeven wundes longe and wide
In twenti stedes and wel mo,   485
Fro the croune til the to.
Hwan he saw that, he was wod,
And was it ferlik, hu he stod,
For the blod ran of his sides
So water that fro welle glides;   490
But thanne bigan he for to mowe
With the barre, and let hem shewe
Hu he cowthe sore smite;
For was ther non, long ne lite,
That he mouhte overtake,   495
That he ne garte his croun krake,
So that on a litel stunde
Feld he twenti to the grund.
Tho bigan gret dine to rise,
For the laddes on ilke wise   500
Him asayleden with grete dintes;
Fro fer he stoden, and with flintes
And gleyves schoten him fro ferne,
For drepen him he wolden yerne.
But dursten he newhen him no more   505
Thanne he bor or leun wore.

481. umbiyeden: MS vn bi yeden
503. and: MS him

477ff. A reference to the medieval sport of bear-baiting: the bear was chained by the neck or hind legs, and dogs set upon him.

491. *mowe:* Havelok lays about him with the door-tree like a mower with his scythe.

502–3. 'They stood at a distance, and shot at him with flints and spears at long range'

Huwe Raven that dine herde,
And thowhte wel that men misferde
With his louerd, for his wif,
And grop an ore and a long knif   510
And thider drof also an hert
And cam ther on a litel stert,
And saw how the laddes wode
Havelok his louerd umbistode,
And beten on him so doth the smith   515
With the hamer on the stith.

'Allas, ' quath Huwe, 'that Y was boren!
That ever et Ich bred of koren!
That Ich here this sorwe se!
Roberd! Willam! hware are ye?   520
Gripeth ether unker a god tre,
And late we nouht thise doges fle,
Til ure louerd wreke [be].
Cometh swithe and folwes me!
Ich have in honde a ful god ore: 525
Datheit hwo ne smite sore!'
'Ya, leve, ya!' quod Roberd sone,
We haven ful god liht of the mone.'
Roberd grop a staf strong and gret,
That mouhte ful wel bere a net,   530
And Willam Wendut grop a tre
Mikel grettere than his the,
And Bernard held his ax ful faste;
I seye was he nouht the laste;

512. cam: MS cham
517. quath Huwe: MS hwat hwe
526. hwo: MS wo
532. the: MS thre

509. A reference to the original motivation of the attack.
521. *ether unker*, 'each of you two'. The second person dual has fallen in under the first person form.
532. *the*, 'thigh', seems a likely emendation.

And lopen forth so he weren wode   535
To the laddes ther he stode,
And yaf hem wundes swithe grete.
Ther mihte men wel se boyes bete,
And ribbes in here sides breke,
And Havelok on hem wel wreke.   540
He broken armes, he broken knes,
He broken shankes, he broken thes.
He dide the blod ther renne dune
To the fet riht from the croune,
For was ther spared heved non: 545
He leyden on hevedes ful god won,
And made croune breke and crake
Of the broune and of the blake.
He maden here backes also bloute
Als here wombes, and made hem rowte   550
Als he weren kradelbarnes:
So dos the child that moder tharnes.
Datheit the recke! for he it servede.
Hwat dide he thore? Weren he werewed!
So longe haveden he but and bet   555
With neves under hernes set,
That of tho sixti men and on
Ne wente ther awey lives non.

On the morwen, hwan it was day,
Ilc on other wirwed lay   560
Als it were dogges that weren henged;

550. here: MS he
559. hwan: MS hhan

---

538. The 'men and boys' imagery is present all through this passage, and
prepares for lines 549–53: 'They made their backs as soft as their bellies, and made
them bawl like babies in their cradles—just like a child who has lost its mother.'

553–4. 'A curse on anyone who cares! They deserved it. What business had
they there? They were mauled.'

556. Literally, 'with fists set under brains'. There is a Norse idiom, *sttja
hnefann á nasar* which means 'to punch on the nose,' and probably this is the
sense here.

And summe leye in dikes slenget,
And summe in gripes bi the her
Drawen ware, and laten ther.

(Havelok's company are now taken into the house of Earl Ubbe: once again the miraculous light is seen to issue from his mouth, and Ubbe recognizes him as the rightful heir. He raises the country against the usurping Godard, who is defeated and put to death. Havelok is crowned king, then returns to England where he quickly recovers Goldeboru's inheritance. Godrich is burnt at the stake, and all Havelok's companions are generously rewarded.)

562-4. 'And some lay in ditches, where they had been thrown, and some had been dragged by the hair to trenches, and left there.'

III. *Floriz and Blauncheflur*

WRITTEN in the second half of the thirteenth century, this is a version of one of the best-known stories of the Middle Ages. The story itself is of eastern origin, bearing strong resemblances to both Arabic and Byzantine love-tales. It may well have reached the West by means of the returning crusaders, or in a written Latin form *via* Constantinople. There seem to have been two versions current in Western Europe, the more original being intended for a sophisticated aristocratic audience, and the other being a popular adaptation of the material. Though the English *Floriz and Blauncheflur* is something of a popularization, it derives from a French version of the first type.

There are four extant MSS, all more or less incomplete. Only the fifteenth-century Egerton MSS preserves the early part of the romance, from which the first extract is taken: the second is printed from the fourteenth-century Cambridge MS which also contains *King Horn*.

MSS: (a) British Museum Egerton 2862; (b) Cambridge University Library Gg.4.27.2

Dialect: South-east Midlands

Edition: King Horn, Floriz and Blauncheflur, etc., ed. G. H. McKnight, E.E.T.S., O.S. 14 (1901)

(A Saracen king attacks a band of pilgrims, which includes a young widow who is with child, and carries her and the other survivors off into Spain. Soon, the widow gives birth to a daughter, Blauncheflur, while on the same day, a son, Floriz, is born to the Saracen queen. The two children grow up together and fall in love, but the king tries to put a stop to this by selling the girl into slavery while Floriz is absent. When he returns, he is told that the girl is dead.)

(205)   Now is the burgays to the king coome
        With the golde and his garysone,
        And hath take the king to wolde
        The selver and the coupe of golde.
        They lete make in a chirche   5
        As swithe feire grave wyrche,

    1. burgays: MS Bugays

---

4. This is the price paid by the slave-traders for Blauncheflur. The cup is elaborately described in the French version: it was won by Eneas in the Siege of Troy. As usual, the description is much reduced in the English adaptation.

And lete ley thereuppone
A new feire peynted stone,
With letters al aboute wryte
With ful muche worshippe.   10
Whoso couth the letters rede,
Thus they spoken and thus they seide:
'Here lyth swete Blaunchefloure
That Florys lovyd paramoure.'
Now Florys hath undernome,   15
And to his fader he is coome.
In his fader halle he is lyght;
His fader him grette anoone ryght,
And his moder, the queen, also,
But unnethes myght he that doo,   20
That he ne asked where his lemman bee;
Nonskyns answere chargeth hee.
So longe he is forth noome,
Into chamber he is coome.
The maydenys moder he asked ryght,   25
'Where is Blauncheflour, my swete wyght?'
'Sir,' she seide, 'forsothe ywys,
I ne woot where she is.'
She bithought hur on that lesyng
That was ordeyned byfoore the king.   30
'Thou gabbest me,' he seyde thoo,
'Thy gabbyng doth me muche woo.
Tel me where my leman be.'
Al wepyng seide thenne shee:
'Sir,' shee seide, 'deede.' 'Deede!' seide he.   35
'Sir,' sche seide, 'for sothe, yee.'
'Allas, when died that swete wyght?'
'Sir, withynne this fourtenyght
The erth was leide hur aboute,

---

22. *chargeth:* perhaps an error for *targeth*, 'waits, delays for', which is the reading of MS Cotton Vitellius D.iii.

31–40. Realistic colloquial dialogue was one of the stylistic innovations of the early French romances: this is quite an effective though simple example of it.

And deed she was for thy love.'   40
Flores, that was so feire and gent,
Sownyd there verament.
The cristen woman began to crye
To Jhesu Crist and Seynt Marye.
The king and the queene herde that crye;   45
Into the chamber they ronne on hye,
And the queene herde her byforne
On sowne the childe that she had borne.
The kinges hert was al in care,
That sawe his sone for love so fare.   50
When he awooke and speke moght,
Sore he wept and sore he syght,
And seide to his moder ywis,
'Lede me there that mayde is.'
Theder they brought him on hyghe;   55
For care and sorow he wolde dyghe.
As sone as he to the grave com,
Sone there behelde he then,
And the letters began to rede
That thus spake and thus seide: 60
'Here lyth swete Blauncheflour,
That Florys lovyd paramoure.'
Thre sithes Florys sownydde nouth:
Ne speke he myght not with mouth.
As sone as he awoke and speke myght,   65
Sore he wept and sore he syght.
'Blauncheflour!' he seide, 'Blauncheflour!
So swete a thing was never in boure.
Of Blauncheflour is that Y meene,

62. paramoure: MS pamoure

41ff. The romance is notable for its extreme emotionalism: the courtly
hero, no less than the heroine, shares in it.

46. 'They ran to the chamber above'

47. *herde:* perhaps an error for 'saw'.

67ff. This kind of analytical monologue, with the apostrophe to Death or
Love, is again a characteristic feature of the courtly romance.

For she was come of good kyne.   70
Lytel and muche loveden the
For thy goodnesse and thy beauté.
Yif deth were dalt aryght,
We shuld be deed both on oo nyght.
On oo day borne we were;   75
We shul be ded both in feere.'
    'Deeth,' he seide, 'ful of envye,
And of alle trechorye,
Refte thou hast me my lemman.
For sothe,' he seide, 'thou art to blame.   80
She wolde have levyd, and thu noldest,
And fayne wolde Y dye, and thu woldest.
[With there me wolde that thou were,
Nul tu no wight come there,
And ther me wolde that thou . . . ne come,   85
Ther thou wolt come ilome.
Thilke that buste best to libbe,
Hem thou stikest under the ribbe,
And yif ther is eni forlived wrecche
That of is live nought ne recche,   90
That fawe wolde deie for sorewe and elde,
On hem neltou nought bi helde.
No lengore Ich nelle mi life bileve,
I chulle be mid hyre ere eve.]
After deeth clepe nomore Y nylle,   95
But slee my self now Y wille.'

(His parents prevent his suicide and tell him the truth, promising to help him
win back Blauncheflur. In disguise, he traces her to the harem of the Emir of
Babylon, where he is given advice by the bridge-keeper of the city, Dariz.)

    85. . . . ne: the MS is illegible at this point

83–94. These lines are not in the Egerton MS: as they develop Floriz's
speech, I have taken them from MS Cotton Vitellius D.iii.
83–6. Perhaps, 'Wherever men wish you to be, there you will by no means
come, and where they wish you to be absent, there you will come often.'
92. 'You will not stand by him.'

(Cambridge MS l. 209)

      'And Babilloine, Ihc understonde,
      Dureth abute furtennight gonde.
      Abute the walle ther buth ate,
      Sevesithe tuenti gates.   100
      And ine the buregh amidde right
      Beoth twe tures ipight.
      Eche day in al the yere
      The feire is ther iliche plenere.
      Seve hundred tures and two   105
      Beoth in the burgh, bithute mo.
      And ine the burgh amidde right
      Beoth twe ture ipight,
      Of lym and of marbleston;
      In the world nis swiche tur non.   110
      In the tur ther is a welle,
      Suthe cler hit is with alle.
      He urneth in o pipe of bras,
      Whider so hit ned was.
      Fram flore into flore   115
      The strimes urneth store,
      Fram bure into halle,
      The strimes of this welle.
      In the tur is o kernel
      Of selver and of crestel.   120
      On the tur anovenon
      Is a charbugleston
      That yiveth leme day and night,
      Ne bi hit nevre so derk night.

97ff. The description of the exotic location is one of the familiar features of romance. The English poet often seems baffled, however, by some of the intricacies of his French original, and the sense is sometimes hard to follow.

98. *i.e.* 'It takes a fortnight to journey round the city walls.'

101-2. Apparently a scribe's anticipation of lines 107-8.

115-18. The domestic and sanitary arrangements of the Saracens were a source of wonder to Western Europe as a result of the Crusades. However, it is not easy to see how this water-system functioned.

119. *kernel:* perhaps *kanel*, 'canal, conduit' (Hausknecht).

In the buregh ne darfe me berne 125
Lampe ne torche ne lanterne,
That he ne yiveth light and leme,
As doth a day the sunne beme.
The porter is prud withalle;
Eche day he goth on the walle, 130
And ef ther cometh eni man
Bithinne thilke barbecan,
Bute he him yeve leve,
He wule him bothe bete and reve.
The porter is culvart and felun: 135
He wule him sette areisun.
Ther buth in the highe tur
Forti maidenes and four.
Wel were that ilke mon
That mighte winne with that on. 140
Ne thorte he never ful iwis
Wilne more of paradis.
Ther buth serjauns in the stage
That serveth the maidenes of parage;
Ac ne mot ther non ben inne 150
That one the breche bereth the ginne,
Nother bi daie ne bi night,
Bute he also capun beo idight.
And the Admiral is such a gume,
In al the world nis such a sune. 155

125-8. 'In the castle there is no need for men to burn a lamp, torch or lantern, (for) it (the carbuncle) gives as much light and brightness as the sun's beams by day.'

135. The vocabulary of French feudal poetry.

141-2. The poem seems to betray its Oriental origins: it is a very Mohammedan picture of Paradise.

151. 'Who carries the tool in his breeches', *i.e.* is sexually able.

153. *i.e.* is a eunuch.

154. *Admiral*, 'Emir' is a borrowing from the Arabic *amir*, 'commander', with the initial *am-* treated as the usual French *am-* from Latin *adm-*; *-al* reflects the fact that the Arabic title was often followed by *al*, 'of the', and this was assumed to be part of the title. It was first used in England of the commander at sea in Edward III's reign.

Ne bu his wife nevre so schene,
Bute o yer ne schal heo beon his quene,
Thegh heo luve him ase hire lif,
That he nele habbe another wif.
And, Floriz, I mai the telle fore,   160
Heo schal beon his quene icore.
Alle the maidenes of parage
Me schal bringe adun of the stage,
And leden hem in to on orchard,
The faireste of al the middelerd.   165
Abute the orchard is a wal;
The ethelikeste ston is cristal.
Ho so wonede a moneth in that spray
Nolde him nevre longen away.
So merie is therinne the fogheles song   170
That joie and blisse is evre among.
In the orchard is a welle
That is suthe cler with alle.
Ihc mai seggen iwis,
The strimes cometh fram paradis.   175
For in the strimes, the smale stones,
Hi beoth ther funden evrech one,
Bothe saphire and sardoines,
And suthe riche cassidoines,
And jacinctes and topaces,   180
And onicle of muchel grace,
And mani on other direwerthe ston
That Ich nu nempne ne can.
Above the walle stent a treo,

158–9. 'Though she loves him as her own life, yet he will take another wife.'

166. The description of the garden is the great set-piece of the courtly French version, and this can still be seen in the English poem, though the passage is less than half the length.

168. *spray:* presumably the common ME sense of 'branch' or 'twig' is here extended to the orchard itself; the meaning 'shower of water' is not recorded until much later.

177–82. Though the catalogue of stones here is probably purely decorative, there is always the possibility of formal symbolism, derived from the lapidaries.

That faireste that mighte in erthe beo.   185
Hit is ihote the treo of luve,
For lef and blosme beoth ther buve.
So sone so the olde beoth idon,
Ther springeth niwe right anon.
Alle thilke that clene maidenes beo   190
Schulle sitte arewe under that treo;
And which falleth on that furste flur
Schal beo quene and fonge thonur.
Yef ther is eni maide forleie,
The wal is of so muchel eie,   195
And heo stepe to the grunde
For to wassche hire honde,
Ha bulmeth up so he were wod,
And chaungeth fram water into blod.
On wuche the welle fareth so,'   200
Also suithe he wurth fordo.

(Floriz succeeds in bribing the porter, and is carried into the harem in a basket of flowers. There he is briefly united with Blauncheflur, before they are discovered in bed together by the Emir. They are tried, and seem on the point of being sentenced to death, when their fairness and constancy to each other touches the Emir's compassion. He knights Floriz and causes the two children to be married. Meanwhile, a messenger arrives with the news of Floriz's father's death, and he and Blauncheflur return to rule the kingdom.)

186-9. Another feature of the Earthly Paradise.

194ff. The well which tests chastity may be one of the marks of Greek influence. Similar situations are found in Byzantine romance, though other explanations are possible.

198. *bulmeth:* unrecorded. Perhaps an error for *welmeth*, 'boils, surges up'.

IV. Sir Orfeo

THIS poem, written about 1300, is one of the small group of English romances which depend or claim to depend upon Breton *lais* (see Introduction, pp. 37–8). Two of the undoubted English *lais*, *Lai le Freine* and *Sir Launfal*, are translated from poems by the twelfth-century French poetess Marie de France, and it seems very probable that *Sir Orfeo* also had an OF source. There are references in twelfth- and thirteenth-century French literature to a Breton *lai* of Orpheus, and Walter Map(*fl.* 1200) in *De Nugis Curialium* recounts a Celtic tale, not unlike our poem, which had been contaminated with the Orpheus story. The primary source is the classical story, familiar in the Middle Ages through the versions of Virgil, Ovid and Boethius, and with this are fused elements of a popular Celtic story-type. The English work is likely to be a faithful translation from French, slightly modified and popularized to suit the needs of a travelling minstrel's audience. It survives in three texts, and I print from the Auchinleck, which is the earliest, and probably the most faithful to the original. The twenty-four-line prologue, of considerable importance to the study of the *lai* form, is supplied from the Harleian MS (early fifteenth century): it is found in the Auchinleck MS as the prologue to *Lai le Freine*.

MSS: (a) British Museum MS Harley 3810; (b) MS Auchinleck W.4.1, National Library of Scotland, Edinburgh

Dialect: Rhymes and vocabulary indicate the south-western part of the Anglian areas; but from a literary point of view, *Sir Orfeo* belongs with the East Midland romances of the late thirteenth and fourteenth centuries. Perhaps written in the London area, in a variety of the Westminster or Middlesex dialect. Auchinleck represents the beginnings of a standard literary dialect based on London: Harley preserves some West Midland features.

Editions: *Sir Orfeo*, ed. A. J. Bliss (Oxford, 1954); see also K. Sisam, *Fourteenth Century Verse and Prose* (Oxford, 1921)

Text: Past participial forms with i/y prefix are hyphenated.

> [We redyn ofte and fynde y-w(ryte)
> As clerkes don us to wyte,

lines 1–24 from Harley
1. y-wryte: last four letters illegible

1–24. The lines would make an adequate prologue to any Breton lay: the account corresponds quite faithfully to that given by Marie de France, though it is probably the original composition of a poet who was well read in poems of this type. Note that a *lai* need not be a romance (line 7).

The layes that ben of harpyng
Ben y-founde of frely thing:
Sum ben of wele, and sum of wo,   5
And sum of joy and merthe also;
Sum of bourdys and sum of rybaudry,
And sum ther ben of the feyré;
Sum of trechery, and sum of gyle,
And sum of happes that fallen by whyle;   10
Of alle thing that men may se
Moost to lowe, forsothe, they be.
In Brytayn this layes arne y-wrytt,
Furst y-founde and forth y-gete,
Of aventures that fallen by dayes   15
Whereof Brytouns made her layes.
When they myght owher heryn
Of aventures that ther weryn,
They toke her harpys with game,
Maden layes and yaf it name.   20
Of aventures that han befalle
Y can sum telle, but nought all:
Herken, lordynges that ben trewe,
And Y wol you telle of Syr Orphewe.]
   Orfeo was a king,   25
In Inglond an heighe lording,
A stalworth man and hardi bo,
Large and curteys he was also.
His fader was comen of King Pluto,

21. aventures: MS avntures
27. A stalworth: MS T stalworth

---

12. *moost to lowe*, 'most (worthy) to be praised'. However, the third MS, Ashmole 61, and the *Lai le Freine* prologue have *most o love*, 'mostly of love', and this, to judge by the plots of surviving lays, may well be the original reading.

26. There is a fairly consistent adaptation of place-names throughout, to give some local application.

29-30. The classical King of Hades came to be regarded as the King of Fairyland, though since the latter plays a prominent part in this tale, the writer seems unaware of the connexion. 'King Juno' is probably a scribe's error.

And his moder of King Juno.   30
That sum time were as godes y-holde
For aventours that thai dede and told.
This king sojournd in Traciens,
That was a cité of noble defens
(For Winchester was cleped tho   35
Traciens, withouten no.)
The king hadde a quen of priis
That was y-cleped Dame Herodis,
The fairest levedi, for the nones,
That might gon on bodi and bones,   40
Ful of love and of godenisse;
Ac no man may telle hir fairnisse.
   Bifel so in the comessing of May,
When miri and hot is the day,
And oway beth winter schours,   45
And everi feld is ful of flours,
And blosme breme on everi bough
Overal wexeth miri anough,
This ich quen, Dame Heurodis,
Tok to maidens of priis,   50
And went in an undrentide
To play bi an orchard-side,
To se the floures sprede and spring,
And to here the foules sing.
Thai sett hem doun al thre   55
Under a fair ympe-tre,

43. Bifel: MS Uifel

---

31. The usual medieval view of the classical gods is euhemeristic.

32. Sisam here inserts fourteen lines from the Harley MS which are probably
original celebrating Orfeo's skill as a harper and his generosity to the profession

33. *Traciens:* Thrace. However, to suit English audiences, this is identified
with Winchester, which, as the old capital of England, becomes the conventional seat of an English king in literature.

56. *ympe-tre,* 'grafted, orchard tree'. It is a commonplace in the *lais* that
those who lie down or sleep under a tree place themselves in the power of the
fairies. The motif seems to be of Celtic origin, and *insula pomorum,* 'the isle of
apples', is one of the names for the Celtic Otherworld.

And wel sone this fair quene
Fel on slepe opon the grene.
The maidens durst hir nought awake,
Bot lete hir ligge and rest take.   60
So sche slepe til afternone,
That undertide was al y-done.
Ac as sone as sche gan awake,
Sche crid, and lothli bere gan make;
Sche froted hir honden and hir fet,   65
And crached hir visage, it bled wete.
Hir riche robe hye al to-rett,
And was reveyd out of hire witt.
The tvo maidens hir biside
No durst with hir no leng abide,   70
Bot ourn to the palays ful right,
And told bothe squier and knight
That her quen awede wold,
And bad hem go and hir at-hold.
Knightes urn and levedis also,   75
Damisels sexti and mo;
In the orchard to the quen hye come,
And her up in her armes nome,
And brought hir to bed atte last,
And held hir there fine fast;   80
Ac ever sche held in o cri,
And wold up and owy.
When Orfeo herd that tiding,
Never him nas wers for nothing.
He come with knightes tene   85
To chaumber, right bifor the quene,
And biheld and seyd with grete pité:
'O lef liif, what is te,

---

68. *reveyd.* The word seems to be the past participle of ME *revey*, 'to hunt
along the banks of a river' (Anglo-Norman *riveier*). The extension of meaning
is straightforward, and 'hunted' or 'driven' gives the sense required: 'and she
was driven out of her wits' (Bliss).
81. 'But she kept up a continuous screaming'
88. *what is te:* 'what ails you?'

That ever yete hast ben so stille,
And now gredest wonder schille?   90
Thi bodi that was so white y-core,
With thine nailes is al to-tore.
Allas! thi rode that was so red
Is al wan, as thou were ded,
And also thine fingres smale   95
Beth al blodi and al pale.
Allas! thi lovesom eyghen to
Loketh so man doth on his fo!
A! dame, Ich biseche merci,
Lete ben al this reweful cri,   100
And tel me what the is, and hou,
And what thing may the help now.'
Tho lay sche stille atte last
And gan to wepe swithe fast,
And seyd thus, the king to: 105
'Allas! mi lord Sir Orfeo,
Sethen we first togider were,
Ones wroth never we nere,
Bot ever Ich have y-loved the
As mi liif, and so thou me.   110
Ac now we mot delen ato.
Do thi best, for Y mot go!'
'Allas!' quath he, 'forlorn Icham!
Whider wiltow go, and to wham?
Whider tho gost, Ichil with the,   115
And whider Y go, thou schalt with me.'
'Nay, nay, sir, that nought nis!
Ichil the telle al hou it is:
As Ich lay this undertide
And slepe under our orchard-side,   120
Ther come to me to fair knightes
Wel y-armed al to rightes,

---

101. 'And tell me what ails you, and how (it came about)'

113. *Icham = Ich am*, similarly *Ichil* (115, 118) = *Ich wille*. These forms continue to be characteristic of Southern dialects until much later.

117. *that nought nis*, 'that cannot be'

And bad me comen an heighing
And speke with her lord the kinge.
And ich answerd at wordes bold,   125
Y no durst nought, no Y nold.
Thai priked ogain as thai might drive.
Tho com her king, also blive,
With an hundred knightes and mo,
And damisels an hundred also,   130
Al on snowe-white stedes.
As white as milke were her wedes:
Y no seighe never yete bifore
So fair creatours y-core.
The king hadde a croun on hed,   135
It nas of silver, no of gold red,
Ac it was of a precious ston,
As bright as the sonne it schon.
And as son as he to me cam,
Wold Ich, nold Ich, he me nam,   140
And made me with him ride
Opon a palfray bi his side,
And brought me to his palays,
Wel atird in ich ways,
And schewed me castels and tours,   145
Rivers, forestes, frith with flours,
And his riche stedes ichon,
And sethen me brought ogain hom
Into our owhen orchard,
And said to me thus afterward: 150
"Loke, dame, tomorwe thatow be
Righte here under this ympe-tre,
And than thou schalt with ous go,
And live with ous evermo;

126. Y no durst: MS Y n durst

---

123. *an heighing*, 'in haste'
143-4. *palays:ways.* The original rhyme was perhaps *palys:wys*, 'wise'
(Sisam).
147. 'and all his rich estates'
D

And yif thou makest ous y-let,   155
Whar thou be, thou worst y-fet,
And to-tore thine limes al,
That nothing help the ne schal.
And thei thou best so to-torn,
Yete thou worst with ous y-born!" '   160
    When King Orfeo herd this cas,
'O we!' quath he, 'allas, allas!
Lever me were to lete mi liif,
Than thus to lese the quen mi wiif!'
He asked conseyl at ich man,   165
Ac no man him help no can.
Amorwe the undertide is come
And Orfeo hath his armes y-nome,
And wele ten hundred knightes with him,
Ich y-armed stout and grim,   170
And with the quen wenten he
Right unto that ympe-tre.
Thai made scheltrom in ich a side,
And sayd thai wold there abide,
And dye ther everichon,   175
Er the quen schuld fram hem gon.
Ac yete amiddes hem ful right
The quen was oway y-tvight,
With fairi forth y-nome;
Me wist never wher sche was bicome.   180
Tho was ther criing, wepe and wo,
The king into his chaumber is go,
And oft swoned opon the ston,
And made swiche diol and swiche mon
That neighe his liif was y-spent;   185
Ther was non amendment.

155-6. 'And if you make us any resistance, wherever you be, you will be fetched.' Some editors gloss *Whar thou be* as 'Beware'.

173. *scheltrom*: a phalanx of infantry, like the Roman *testudo*—the Anglo-Saxon battle-formation.

177-8. Note the effective contrast between the elaborate preparations for the defence of the queen, and the speed which with her abduction is described.

He cleped togider his barouns,
Erls, lordes of renouns,
And when thai al y-comen were,
'Lordinges,' he said, 'bifor you here   190
Ich ordainy min heighe steward
To wite mi kingdom afterward.
In mi stede ben he schal
To kepe mi londes overal.
For now Ichave mi quen y-lore,   195
The fairest levedi that ever was bore,
Never eft Y nil no woman se.
Into wildernes Ichil te,
And live ther ever more
With wilde bestes in holtes hore.   200
And when ye understond that Y be spent,
Make you than a parlement,
And chese you a newe king.
Now doth your best with al mi thing!'
  Tho was ther wepeing in the halle,   205
And grete cri among hem alle.
Unnethe might old or yong
For wepeing speke a word with tong.
Thai kneled adoun al y-fere
And praid him, yif his wille were,   210
That he no schuld nought fram hem go.
'Do way!' quath he, 'It schal be so!'
Al his kingdom he forsoke,
Bot a sclavin on him he toke.
He no hadde kirtel no hode,   215
Schert no nother gode,
Bot his harp he tok algate,
And dede him barfot out atte gate;
No man most with him go.

205. Tho: MS Lo

187–8. *barouns:renouns* Forms like *renouns* in rhyme are usually taken over from a French original (Sisam).
202. 'Make a parliament for yourselves'. A borrowing from English practice?

O, way! what, ther was wepe and wo,   220
When he that hadde ben king with croune
Went so poverlich out of toun!
Thurch wode and over heth
Into the wilderness he geth.
Nothing he fint that him is ays,   225
Bot ever he liveth in gret malais.
He that hadde y-werd the fowe and griis,
And on bed the purper biis,
Now on hard hethe he lith,
With leves and gresse he him writh.   230
He that hadde had castels and tours,
River, forest, frith with flours,
Now, thei it comenci to snewe and frese,
This king mot make his bed in mese.
He that had y-had knightes of priis   235
Bifor him kneland, and levedis,
Now seth he no thing that him liketh,
Bot wilde wormes bi him striketh.
He that had y-had plenté
Of mete and drink, of ich deynté,   240
Now may he alday digge and wrote
Er he finde his fille of rote.
In somer he liveth bi wild frut,
And berien bot gode lite:
In winter may he nothing finde   245
Bot rote, grases and the rinde.

244. berien: MS berren

---

227. *the fowe and griis*. This is a partial translation of the OF phrase, *vair et gris*. *Vair* is parti-coloured fur, made of alternate pieces of the grey back and white belly of the squirrel, and is rendered by *fowe* from OE *fāg*, 'varicolour'. *Gris* is the grey fur alone. Note the rhyme with *biis* which was probably in the French original.

239ff. Orpheus's life in the wilderness derives ultimately from classical sources, but the description may have been influenced by Celtic tradition—for example, the accounts of Merlin Silvestris in poems such as Geoffrey of Monmouth's *Vita Merlini*.

244. 'and berries, of little worth as food'

Al his bodi was oway duine
For missays, and al to-chine.
Lord! who may telle the sore
This king sufferd ten yere and more?   250
His here of his berd, blac and rowe,
To his girdel-stede was growe.
His harp, whereon was al his gle,
He hidde in an holwe tre,
And when the weder was clere and bright,   255
He toke his harp to him wel right,
And harped al his owhen wille.
Into alle the wode the soun gan schille,
That alle the wilde bestes that ther beth
For joie abouten him thai teth,   260
And alle the foules that ther were
Come and sete on ich a brere
To here his harping a-fine,
So miche melody was therein;
And when he his harping lete wold,   265
No best bi him abide nold.

   He might se him bisides.
Oft in hot undertides,
The king of fairy with his rout
Com to hunt him al about,   270
With dim cri and bloweing,
And houndes also with him berking;
Ac no best thai no nome,
Ne never he nist whider thai bi-come.

247–8. 'His body was quite wasted away on account of his hardships, and all scarred.'

267ff. The fairy army and the fairy hunt are well-established features of Celtic folklore. Walter Map (*op. cit.*) gives several instances of the appearance of the fairy host, and also has a curious story of the hunt.

271. *dim:* clearly the MS reading. From the other MSS it seems clear that the original read *dune* or *dine* (OE *dyne*), 'noise'. Aesthetically, however, the Auchinleck reading, whether emendation or error, is most acceptable.

273. Note the distinction drawn between the fairies and their human captives: the fairies take no beasts in their hunting, but when the troop of ladies loose their falcons, each kills his prey (295–9).

And other while he might him se   275
As a gret ost bi him te,
Wel atourned, ten hundred knightes,
Ich y-armed to his rightes,
Of cuntenance stout and fers,
With mani desplaid baners,   280
And ich his swerd y-drawe hold,
Ac never he nist whider thai wold.
And other while he seighe other thing:
Knightes and levedis com daunceing
In queynt atire, gisely,   285
Queynt pas and softly,
Tabours and trumpes yede hem bi,
And al maner menstraci.
    And on a day he seighe him biside
Sexti levedis on hors ride,   290
Gentil and jolif as brid on ris,
Nought o man amonges hem ther nis.
And ich a faucoun on hond bere,
And riden on haukin bi o rivere.
Of game thai founde wel god haunt,   295
Maulardes, hayroun and cormeraunt;
The foules of the water ariseth,
The faucouns hem wele deviseth;
Ich faucoun his pray slough.
That seigh Orfeo and lough: 300
'Parfay!' quath he, 'Ther is fair game;
Thider Ichil, bi Godes name!
Ich was y-won swiche werk to se.'
He aros, and thider gan te.
To a levedi he was y-come,   305
Biheld, and hath wele undernome,
And seth bi al thing that it is
His owhen quen, Dam Heurodis.
Yern he biheld hir, and sche him eke,
Ac noither to other a word no speke.   310
For messais that sche on him seighe,
That had ben so riche and so heighe,

The teres fel out of her eighe.
The other levedis this y-seighe
And maked hir oway to ride: 315
Sche most with him no lenger abide.
'Allas!' quath he, 'Now me is wo!
Whi nil deth now me slo?
Allas! wroche, that Y no might
Dye now after this sight!   320
Allas! to long last mi liif,
When Y no dar nought with mi wiif,
No hye to me, o word speke.
Allas! whi nil min hert breke?
Parfay!' quath he, 'tide wat bitide,   325
Whider-so this levedis ride,
The selve way Ichil streche;
Of liif no deth me no reche.'
His sclavin he ded on also spac,
And heng his harp opon his bac,   330
And had wel gode wil to gon.
He ne spard noither stub no ston.
In at a roche the levedis rideth,
And he after and nought abideth.
When he was in the roche y-go   335
Wele thre mile, other mo,
He com into a fair contray,
As bright so sonne on somers day,
Smothe and plain and al grene,
Hille no dale nas ther non y-sene.   340
Amidde the lond a castel he sighe,
Riche and real and wonder heighe.
Al the utmast wal
Was clere and schine as cristal.

309–16. I follow Sisam's punctuation here, except for replacing the comma after 315 with a colon. Bliss puts a full stop after 312, and argues that Orfeo and Heurodis do not speak to each other, not because of an enchantment, but because Heurodis is overcome with emotion at the sight of Orfeo. But later (321–3) Orfeo says they dared not speak, seeming to imply some prohibition.
328. 'I care neither for life nor death.'

An hundred tours ther were about,   345
Degiselich, and baraild stout;
The butras com out of the diche,
Of rede gold y-arched riche.
The vousour was avowed al
Of ich maner divers aumal.   350
Within ther wer wide wones,
Al of precious stones;
The werst piler on to biholde
Was al of burnist gold.
Al that lond was ever light,   355
For whan it schuld be therk and night,
The riche stones light gonne
As bright as doth at none the sonne.
No man may telle, no thenche in thought
The riche werk that ther was wrought.   360
Bi al thing him think that it is
The proude court of Paradis.
In this castel the levedis alight;
He wold in after, yif he might.
  Orfeo knokketh atte gate;   365
The porter was redi therate
And asked what he wold have y-do.
'Parfay!' quath he, 'Icham a minstrel, lo!
To solas thi lord with mi gle,
Yif his swete wille be.'   370

346ff. Orfeo's entry through the rock is very similar to the story told by Walter Map of the British king, Herla, and the details of the description of the Otherworld occur again and again in Celtic legend—the crystal wall, the pillar of gold or silver, etc.

347-8. The flying buttress was scarcely known in England in the thirteenth century: the detail seems to suggest an OF original.

349. *avowed*. No editor has succeeded in accounting for this form, though the meaning 'decorated, adorned' seems inescapable. Bliss suggests a hypothetical OE *āfāgod (fāgian) might produce it in this dialect.

350. *aumal*, 'enamel'. So Bliss, and this looks to be the MS reading, though previous editors have printed *animal*.

356. *therk*, 'dark', from unrecorded OE *theorc, appears in ME to be restricted to the East Midlands.

The porter undede the gate anon
And lete him into the castel gon.
   Than he gan bihold about al,
And seighe ful liggeand within the wal
Of folk that were thider y-brought,   375
And thought ded and nere nought.
Sum stode withouten hade,
And sum non armes nade,
And sum thurh the bodi hadde wounde,
And sum lay wode, y-bounde.   380
And sum armed on hors sete,
And sum astrangled as thai ete,
And sum were in water adreynt,
And sum with fire al forshreynt;
Wives ther lay on childbedde,   385
Sum ded and sum awedde,
And wonder fele ther lay bisides,
Right as thai slepe her undertides.
Eche was thus in this warld y-nome,
With fairi thider y-come.   390
Ther he seighe his owhen wiif,
Dame Heurodis, his lef liif,
Slepe under an ympe-tre:
Bi her clothes he knewe that it was he.
   And when he hadde bihold this mervaile alle,   395
He went into the kinges halle.
Than seighe he ther a semly sight,
A tabernacle blisseful and bright,
Therin her maister king sete,

392. lef liif: MS liif liif

---

374. *ful liggeand*. The line seems corrupt. Probably *ful* is superfluous, though Sisam suggests emending it to *fele*, 'a great number'.

376. 'And seemed dead, yet were not.' The Celtic and classical sources of the poem seem to have produced some confusion here. The Celtic Otherworld is the land of the living, and many of the figures here, including Heurodis, have been carried off alive. The majority, though, are fixed in the moment of death, as in the classical legend.

D*

And her quen fair and swete.   400
Her crounes, her clothes, schine so bright
That unnethe bihold he hem might.
When he hadde biholden al that thing,
He kneled adoun bifor the king:
'O lord,' he seyd, 'yif it thi wille were,   405
Mi menstraci thou schust y-here.'
The king answerd: 'What man artow,
That art hider y-comen now?
Ich, no none that is with me,
No sent never after the.   410
Sethen that Ich here regni gan,
Y no fond never so fole-hardi man
That hider to ous durst wende,
Bot that Ic him wald ofsende.'
'Lord,' quath he, 'trowe ful wel,   415
Y nam bot a pover menstrel;
And, sir, it is the maner of ous
To seche mani a lordes hous:
Thei we nought welcom no be,
Yete we mot proferi forth our gle.'   420
    Bifor the king he sat adoun,
And tok his harp so miri of soun,
And trempeth his harp as he wele can,
And blisseful notes he ther gan,
That al that in the palays were   425
Com to him forto here,
And liggeth adoun to his fete,
Hem thinketh his melody so swete.
The king herkneth and sitt ful stille;
To here his gle he hath gode wille.   430
Gode bourde he hadde of his gle;
The riche quen also hadde he.
When he hadde stint his harping,
Than seyd to him the king:

---

414. 'unless I had sent for him'
432. *hadde he*, 'had she'.

'Menstrel, me liketh wele thi gle.   435
Now aske of me what it be,
Largelich Ichil the pay.
Now speke, and tow might assay.'
'Sir,' he seyd, 'Ich biseche the
Thatow woldest yive me   440
That ich levedi bright on ble,
That slepeth under the ympe-tre.'
'Nay,' quath the king, 'that nought nere!
A sori couple of you it were,
For thou art lene, rowe and black,   445
And sche is lovesome, withouten lac.
A lothlich thing it were, forthi,
To sen hir in thi compayni.'
   'O sir!' he seyd, 'Gentil king!
Yete were it a wele fouler thing   450
To here a lesing of thi mouthe:
So, sir, as ye seyd nouthe,
What Ich wold aski, have Y schold,
And nedes thou most thi word hold.'
The king seyd: 'Sethen it is so,   455
Take hir bi the hond and go.
Of hir Ichil thatow be blithe!'
He kneled adoun and thonked him swithe,
His wiif he tok bi the hond,
And dede him swithe out of that lond,   460
And went him out of that thede.
Right as he come the wey he yede.
So long he hath the way y-nome,
To Winchester he is y-come,
That was his owhen cité;   465
Ac no man knewe that it was he.

436. aske: MS alke

---

436. 'Now ask of me whatever you like.' The rash promises of an unwary king are often the centre of medieval romance plots.
444. 'You two would be a very ill-matched pair.'

No forther than the tounes ende
For knoweleche no durst wende,
But with a begger, y-bilt ful narwe,
Ther he tok his herbarwe,   470
To him and to his owhen wiif,
As a minstrel of pover liif,
And asked tidinges of that lond,
And who the kingdom held in hond.
The pover begger in his cote   475
Told him everich a grot,
Hou her quen was stole owy
Ten yer gon, with fairy,
And hou her king en exile yede,
Bot no man wist in wiche thede.   480
And hou the steward the lond gan hold,
And other mani thinges him told.
    Amorwe, ogain nonetide,
He maked his wiif ther abide.
The beggers clothes he borwed anon,   485
And heng his harp his rigge opon,
And went him into that cité,
That men might him biholde and se.
Erles and barouns bold,
Burjays and levedis him gan bihold: 490
'Lo,' thai seyd, 'swiche a man!
Hou long the here hongeth him opan!
Lo, hou his berd hongeth to his kne!
He is y-clongen also a tre!'
And as he yede in the strete,   495

467–8. 'He dared not go further than the city limits, for fear of being recognized.'

469. *y-bilt* qualifies the 'house' implicit in the preposition *with*, thus: 'He took his lodging at the house of a beggar, very incommodiously built' (Bliss).

479. *en exile*. This complete French phrase may give evidence of a French original, but many such phrases were taken over entire into Middle English.

485. This detail is not found in the other MSS, and indeed it seems redundant: after ten years in the wilderness, Orfeo would hardly need to borrow a beggar's disguise.

With his steward he gan mete,
And loude he sett on him a crie:
'Sir steward,' he seyd, 'merci!
Icham an harpour of hethenisse;
Help me now in this distresse!' 500
The steward seyd: 'Com with me, come!
Of that Ichave thou schalt have some.
Everich gode harpour is welcom me to
For mi lordes love, Sir Orfeo.'
In the castel the steward sat atte mete, 505
And mani lording was bi him sete.
Ther were trompours and tabourers,
Harpours fele, and crouders;
Miche melody thai maked alle,
And Orfeo sat stille in the halle 510
And herkneth; when thai ben al stille
He toke his harp and tempred schille.
The blissefulest notes he harped there
That ever ani man y-herd with ere.
Ich man liked wele his gle: 515
The steward biheld, and gan y-se,
And knewe that harp als blive.
'Menstrel,' he seyd, 'so mot thou thrive,
Where hadestow this harp, and hou?
Y pray that thou me telle now.' 520
    'Lord,' quath he, 'in uncouthe thede,
Thurth a wilderness as Y yede,
Ther Y founde in a dale,
With lyouns a man to-torn smale,
And wolves him frete with teth so scharp. 525
Bi him Y fond this ich harp,
Wele ten yere it is y-go.'
'O!' quath the steward, 'now is me wo!

507. trompours: MS trompour

---

508. *crouders*, 'fiddlers'. The word comes from the Welsh *crwth*, a kind of fiddle.
524. 'a man torn to pieces by lions'

That was mi lord, Sir Orfeo!
Allas! wreche, what schal Y do,   530
That have swiche a lord y-lore?
A, way that Ich was y-bore,
That him was so hard grace y-yarked,
And so vile deth y-marked!'
Adoun he fel aswon to grounde: 535
His barouns him tok up in that stounde,
And telleth him hou it geth:
'It nis no bote of mannes deth.'
    King Orfeo knewe wele bi than
His steward was a trewe man   540
And loved him as he aught to do,
And stont up and seyd thus: 'Lo!
Steward, herkne now this thing:
Yif Ich were Orfeo the king,
And hadde y-suffred ful yore   545
In wildernisse miche sore,
And hadde y-won mi quene owy
Out of the lond of fairy,
And hadde y-brought the levedi hende
Right here to the tounes ende,   550
And with a begger her in y-nome,
And were miself hider y-come
Poverlich to the, thus stille,
For to asay thi gode wille,
And Ich founde the thus trewe,   555
Thou schust it never rewe.
Sikerlich, for love, or ay,
Thou schust be king after mi day;

---

537. *hou it geth:* the contemporary idiom 'That's how it goes' expresses this line as well as anything.

538. 'There is no remedy for man's death'—a fairly common ME proverb.

542. The syntax here contributes to the situation: the steward's gradual comprehension of the truth being paralleled by the long succession of conditional clauses.

551. Perhaps 'and (had) taken her into the house of a beggar'. Bliss suggests emending *her* to *were*, paralleling the construction in 552: 'and had been taken in . . .'.

And yif thou of mi deth hadest ben blithe,
Thou schust have voided also swithe.'   560
   Tho al tho that therin sete
That it was King Orfeo underyete,
And the steward him wele knewe:
Over and over the bord he threwe,
And fel adoun to his fet,   565
So dede everich lord that ther sete,
And al thai seyd at o criing:
'Ye beth our lord, sir, and our king!'
Glad thai were of his live;
To chaumber thai ladde him als blive,   570
And bathed him, and schaved his berd,
And tired him as a king apert,
And sethen with gret processioun
Thai brought the quen into the toun,
With al maner menstraci.   575
Lord! ther was grete melody!
For joie thai wepe with her eighe
That hem so sounde y-comen seighe.
Now King Orfeo newe coround is,
And his quen, Dame Heurodis,   580
And lived long afterward,
And sethen was king the steward.
Harpours in Bretaine after than
Herde hou this mervaile bigan,
And made herof a lay of gode likeing,   585
And nempned it after the king.
That lay 'Orfeo' is y-hote:
Gode is the lay, swete is the note.
Thus com Sir Orfeo out of his care:
God graunt ous alle wele to fare! Amen.   590

Explicit

---

560. 'You would have been dismissed on the spot.'
  583ff. Note the importance of the musical setting, in the characteristic reference to the *lai* form.

V. Amis and Amiloun

AGAIN an example of a very popular medieval story, *Amis and Amiloun* dates from the end of the thirteenth century, and is written in a form of the tail-rhyme stanza so common in English medieval romance. There are many surviving treatments of the theme, the life-long devotion of two sworn brothers, and they fall, roughly, into two groups: one, including this poem, in which friendship is seen in the light of a secular ideal of knighthood, and a hagiographic group, which celebrates the Christian virtues of the heroes, illustrating them by miracles and ultimate martyrdom. The original of both groups appears to be an eleventh-century French poem, in the form of a *chanson de geste*: the English poem derives, it seems probable, from an early Anglo-French version, now lost. Four MSS preserve the poem: I print from the Auchinleck MS (the earliest) with some thirty lines supplied from the Egerton MS.

MSS: (a) MS Auchinleck W.4.1, National Library of Scotland, Edinburgh;
(b) British Museum MS Egerton 2862
Dialect: Commonly allotted to North-eastern Midlands, though Trounce definitely places it in East Anglia (see Introduction, p. 24)
Edition: Amis and Amiloun, ed. MacEdward Leach, E.E.T.S., O.S.203 (1937)

(Born on the same day, and identical in appearance, Amis and Amiloun become sworn brothers while serving at the court of the duke. The steward is envious of them, and waits to do them an injury. His chance comes when, Amiloun having been called home, the duke's daughter Belisaunt becomes infatuated with Amis and seduces him. The steward discovers this and denounces Amis to the duke. Amis asks for trial by battle, but is troubled by the prospect of having to swear a false oath. But Amiloun has a presentiment of all this, and arrives back in time to take Amis's place and kill the steward in the combat, in spite of hearing an angel warn him that he will be smitten by leprosy for undertaking an unjust quarrel. Amis marries Belisaunt and succeeds to the dukedom, but Amiloun does become a leper as prophesied, and his wife drives him out, first from his castle and eventually from the country. As he begs his living, his only companion is his nephew, Owain. At last, after many hardships, they arrive at Amis's castle, unaware, with Owain carrying Amiloun on his back. Here, he is finally recognized by his last possession, one of the gold cups which the two friends had exchanged in their youth. Amis bears his friend into the castle, and he and his wife put him to bed and care for him. At the end of a year, an angel appears to Amis in a dream.)

(2197) So it bifel opon a night,
        As Sir Amis, that gentil knight,
        In slepe thought as he lay,
        An angel com fram heven bright
        And stode biforn his bed ful right   5
        And to him thus gan say:
        Yif he wald rise on Cristes morn,
        Swiche time as Jhesu Crist was born,
        And slen his children tvay,
        And alien his (brother) with the blode,   10
        Thurch godes grace, that is so gode,
        His wo schuld wende oway.

        Thus him thought al tho thre night
        An angel out of heven bright
        Warned him ever more   15
        Yif he wald do as he him hight,
        His brother schuld ben as fair a knight
        As ever he was biforn.
        Ful blithe was Sir Amis tho,
        Ac for his childer him was ful wo,   20
        For fairer ner non born.
        Wel loth him was his childer to slo,
        And wel lother his brother forgo,
        That is so kinde ycorn.

        Sir Amiloun met that night also   25
        That an angel warned him tho,
        And seyd to him ful yare,
        Yif his brother wald his childer slo,
        The hert blod of hem to
        Might bring him out of care.   30

        10. brother: MS (b)—MS (a) reads childer

13ff. Note the marked repetition of vocabulary and phrasing: a feature, and often a weakness, of the tail-rhyme stanza.

25. Amiloun does not have this dream in the surviving French versions of the story: its introduction ought to give further psychological depth to the situation, but it is not very intelligently handled.

Amorwe Sir Amis was ful hende
And to his brother he gan wende
And asked him of his fare;
And he him answered ogain ful stille,
'Brother, Ich abide her godes wille,   35
For Y may do na mare.'

Al so thai sete togider thare
And speke of aventours, as it ware,
Tho knightes hende and fre,
Than seyd Sir Amiloun ful yare,   40
'Brother, Y nil nought spare
To tel the in privite,
Me thought tonight in mi sweven
That an angel com fram heven;
For sothe, he told me   45
That thurch the blod of [thin] children to
Y might aschape out of mi wo,
Al hayl and hole to be!'

Than thought the douk, withouten lesing,
For to slen his childer so ying,   50
It were a dedli sinne;
And than thought he, bi heven king,
His brother out of sorwe bring,
For that nold he nought blinne.
So it bifel on Cristes night,   55
Swiche time as Jhesu, ful of might,
Was born to save mankunne,
To chirche to wende, al that ther wes,

46. thin: MS (b)—MS (a) reads min

52–4. 'And then he thought, by the King of Heaven, that he would stop at
nothing to put an end to his brother's misery.'

55ff. There is no mention of Christmas in the extant French versions, and in
them the whole episode is flatly narrated.

58–9. 'All who were there made ready to go to church'. Attendance to
religious duties is usually no more than a part of the normal social background
in romance: religion is, however, insisted on rather more than usual here.

Thai dighten him, withouten les,
With joie and worldes winne. 60

Than thai were redi for to fare,
The douk bad al that ther ware,
To chirche thai schuld wende,
Litel and michel, lasse and mare,
That non bileft in chaumber thare, 65
As thai wald ben his frende,
And seyd he wald himselve that night
Kepe his brother, that gentil knight,
That was so god and kende.
Than was ther non that durst say nay; 70
To chirche thai went in her way,
At hom bileft tho hende.

The douke wel fast gan aspie
The kays of the noricerie,
Er than thai schuld gon. 75
And priveliche he cast his eighe
And aparceived ful witterlye
Where that thai hadde hem don.
And when thai were to chirche went,
Than Sir Amis, verrament, 80
Was bileft alon.
He tok a candel fair and bright
And to the kays he went ful right
And tok hem oway ichon.

Alon himself, withouten mo, 85
Into the chaumber he gan to go,
Ther that his childer were,
And biheld hem bothe to,
Hou fair thai lay togider tho
And slepe both yfere. 90
Than seyd himselve, 'Bi Seyn Jon,
It were gret rewethe you to slon
That God hath bought so dere!'

His kniif he had drawen that tide,
For sorwe he sleynt oway biside   95
And wepe with reweful chere.

Than he hadde wopen ther he stode,
Anon he turned ogain his mode
And sayd withouten delay,
'Mi brother was so kinde and gode,   100
With grimly wounde he schad his blod
For mi love opon a day;
Whi schuld Y than mi childer spare,
To bring mi brother out of care?
O certes,' he seyd, 'nay!   105
To help mi brother now at this nede,
God graunt me thereto wele to spede,
And Mari, that best may!'

No lenger stint he no stode,
Bot hent his kniif with dreri mode   110
And tok his children tho;
For he nold nought spille her blode,
Over a bacine fair and gode
Her throtes he schar atvo.
And when he hadde hem both slain,   115
He laid hem in her bed ogaine—
No wonder thei him were wo—
And hilde hem, that no wight schuld se,
As noman hadde at hem be;
Out of chaumber he gan go.   120

And when he was out of chaumber gon,

---

95. *sleynt*: this could represent the preterite of OE *slencan*, 'to slink, creep', or possibly ON *slyngva*, 'to sling, hurl'. If the latter, Amis throws away the knife, but this seems less likely in the context than that he creeps away from the bed in his remorse.

108. *that best may*, 'that best of maidens'

121ff. Amis's precautions here are difficult to explain in terms of the poem's intention: they look simply realistic—and criminal.

The dor he steked stille anon
As fast as it was biforn;
The kays he hidde under a ston
And thought thai schulde wene ichon 125
That thai hadde ben forlorn.
To his brother he went him than,
And seyd to that careful man,
'Swiche time as God was born,
Ich have the brought mi childer blod, 130
Ich hope it shal do the gode
As the angel seyd biforn.'

'Brother,' Sir Amiloun gan to say,
'Hastow slayn thine children tvay?
Allas, whi destow so?' 135
He wepe and seyd, 'Wailaway!
Ich had lever til domesday
Have lived in care and wo!'
Than seyd Sir Amis, 'Be now still;
Jhesu, when it is his wille, 140
May send me childer mo.
For me of blis thou art al bare;
Ywis, mi liif wil Y nought spare,
To help the now therfro.'

He tok that blode, that was so bright, 145
And alied that gentil knight,
That er was hend in hale,
And sethen in bed him dight
And wreighe him wel warm, aplight,
With clothes riche and fale. 150

129–30. 'On such time as God was born, I have brought you my children's blood'. The Christmas setting is used to some effect.

133ff. Amiloun's astonished grief here would be more effective had the English poet not made him recount his dream to Amis: it might be considered a hint.

145ff. In the French versions, Amiloun is cured immediately, and goes with Amis to the church where Belisaunt is praying.

'Brother,' he seyd, 'ly now stille
And falle on slepe thurch Godes wille,
   As the angel told in tale;
And Ich hope wele withouten lesing
Jhesu, that is heven king,   155
   Schal bote the of thi bale.'

Sir Amis let him ly alon
And into his chapel he went anon,
   In gest as ye may here,
And for his childer, that he hadde slon,   160
To God of heven he made his mon
   And preyd with rewely chere,
Schuld save him fram schame that day,
And Mari, His moder, that best may,
   That was Him leve and dere;   165
And Jhesu Crist, in that stede,
Ful wele he herd that knightes bede
   And graunt him his praiere.

Amorwe astite as it was day,
The levedi com home al with play   170
   With knightes ten and five;
Thai sought the kays ther thei lay;
Thai founde hem nought, thai were oway,
   Wel wo was hem o live.
The douk bad al that ther was   175
Thai schuld hold hem still in pes,
   And stint of her strive,
And seyd he hadde the keys nome,
Schuld noman in the chaumber come
   Bot himself and his wive.   180

---

159. *gest.* It would be interesting to know if this term is significantly used. The original form of the story is a *chanson de geste*, but in the Egerton MS *gest* is replaced by *roumance*.

163. Supply 'that God . . .'. Note that Amis prays to be preserved 'from shame', not directly for the children to be restored to life.

Anon he tok his levedi than
And seyd to hir, 'Leve leman,
Be blithe and glad of mode;
For bi Him that this world wan,
Bothe mi childer Ich have slan,   185
That were so hende and gode;
For me thought in mi sweven
That an angel com fram heven
And seyd me, thurch her blode
Mi brother schuld pass out of his woe;   190
Therfore Y slough hem bothe to,
To hele that frely fode.'

Than was the levedi ferly wo
And seigh hir lord was also;
Sche comfort him ful yare;   195
'O lef liif,' sche seyd tho,
'God may sende ous childer mo,
Of hem have thou no care.
Yif it ware at min hert rote,
For to bring thi brother bote,   200
[My lyf Y wold not spare.
Shal noman oure children see,
Tomorrow shal they beryed bee
As they faire ded ware!'

Thus the lady faire and bryght   205
Comfort hur lord with all hur myght,
As ye mow understonde;
And seth they went both ful ryght
To Sir Amylion, that gentyl knyght,

201. At this point the Auchinleck copy fails, and I follow the Egerton MS.

182ff. The briskness of Amis's confession makes for bathos: however, realism is not aimed at. According to the laws of chivalric friendship, Amis has taken the right course, and again according to those laws, his wife must consent.
192. 'to heal that worthy bold (man).'
204. 'As though they had died naturally'

That ere was free to fonde.   210
When Sir Amylion wakyd thoo,
Al his fowlehed was agoo
Through grace of Goddes sonde;
Than was he as feire a man
As ever he was yet or than,   215
Seth he was born in londe.

Than were they al blith,
Her joy couth noman kyth,
They thonked God that day.
As ye mow listen and lyth,   220
Into a chamber they went swyth,
Ther the children lay;
Without wemme and wound,
Hool and sound the children found,
And layen togeder and play.   225
For joye they wept, there they stood,
And thanked God with myld mood,
Her care was al away.]

(After the rejoicing, Amis and Amiloun return with an army to Amiloun's
country, where they find his evil wife about to marry again. They defeat her
forces in battle, and Amiloun has her confined in a little hut, on bread and
water. He makes Owain lord of the country and goes back with Amis. After
many years, the two die on the same day, and are buried together in the abbey
they have built.)

228. away: supplied from another MS: MS (b) has agoo

---

210. *free to fonde*, 'noble in the proving' (MacEdward Leach)—referring to
Amiloun's previous sacrifice for Amis, presumably. Perhaps, though, *to fonde*
has the sense of 'to search for knightly adventures'.

224. Supply *they* as subject.

225. In other versions of the story, the children are variously playing with
an apple, a ball, the rays of sunlight.

VI. The Gest Hystoriale of the Destruction of Troy

ONE of the many medieval poems on the Trojan War, *The Destruction of Troy* is a free verse paraphrase, made in the north-west of England in about 1375, of the prose *Historia Troiana* (1287) of Guido de Columna. The story of Troy, as represented here, is not that familiar to us from Homer, but derives from the narratives of 'Dares Phrygius' and 'Dictys Cretensis' which first appear in Latin form in the fourth and fifth centuries. These served first as the source for Benoit de Saint-Maure's *Roman de Troie* (*c*. 1184) which in turn was the seminal work for Guido, and for most of the medieval Troy Books. *The Destruction of Troy* is not a romance, but a voluminous verse-chronicle, written as history, but with a strong epic spirit. The prologue, however, which is printed below, gives some insight into the medieval attitude towards narrative fiction and literary form.

Only one MS is extant.

MS: Hunterian Museum, Glasgow
Dialect: Predominantly North-west Midland, with Northern forms
Edition: *The Gest Hystoriale of the Destruction of Troy,* edd. D. Donaldson, G. A. Panton, E.E.T.S., O.S. 39, 56 (1869–74). For this passage, see K. Sisam, *op. cit.*

> Maistur in magesté, Maker of alle,
> Endles and on, ever to laste!
> Now, God, of this grace, graunt me Thi helpe,
> And wysshe me with wyt this werke for to ende
> Of aunters ben olde of aunsetris nobill,   5
> And slydyn uppon shlepe by slomeryng of age;
> Of stithe men in stoure, strongest in armes,
> And wisest in wer, to wale in hor tyme,
> That ben drepit with deth, and there day paste,
> And most out of mynd for there mecull age.   10

---

4 *wysshe = wisse,* 'guide'. Final *sh* was pronounced *ss* in the North: in spelling the process was sometimes reversed.

6. 'and fallen into oblivion through the sleep of ages'

7–8. *Strongest . . . and wisest . . . to wale,* 'the strongest . . . and wisest . . . that could be chosen'.

Soth stories ben stoken up, and straught out of mynde,
And swolowet into swym by swiftenes of yeres,
For new that ben now next at our hond,
Brevyt into bokes for boldyng of hertes,
On lusti to loke with lightnes of wille,   15
Chevyt throughe chaunce and chaungyng of peopull;
Sum tru for to traist, triet in the ende,
Sum feynit o fere and ay false under.

Yche wegh as he will warys his tyme,
And has lykyng to lerne that him list after.   20
But olde stories of stithe that astate helde
May be solas to sum that it segh never,
Be writyng of wees that wist it in dede,
With sight for to serche of hom that suet after,
To ken all the crafte how the case felle   25
By lokyng of letturs that lefte were of olde.

Now of Troy for to telle is myn entent evyn,
Of the stoure and the stryffe when it distroyet was.
Thof fele yeres bene faren syn the fight endid,
And it mevyt out of mynd, myn hit I thinke,   30
Alss wise men have writen the wordes before,
Left it in Latyn for lernyng of us.

But sum poyetis full prist that put hom therto
With fablis and falshed fayned there speche,

11–18. There seems to be a distinction drawn between the old 'true' epic stories and the new fictional romance tales. Veracity is the ultimate criterion in all cases.

15. *on lusti to loke*, 'pleasant to look upon'—an implication that the new stories are entertainment: the old also edify.

21ff. The syntax is very loose, and typical of the limitations of the alliterative style in all but the best hands. The sense is: 'But old stories of the valiant (men) who held high rank may please some who never witnessed their deeds, through the writings of men who knew them at first hand, (which remained) to be examined by those who followed after, in order to make known all the manner in which the events happened, by looking at writings that were left behind of old.'

33–5. Poets should not invent or falsify their material: that is not their *maister* (trade).

And made more of that mater than hom maister were. 35
Sum lokyt over little, and limpit of the sothe.
Amonges that menye, to myn hym be nome,
Homer was holden haithill of dedis
Qwiles his dayes enduret, derrist of other,
That with the Grekys was gret, and of Grice comyn. 40
He feynet myche fals was never before wroght,
And turnet the truth, trust ye non other.
Of his trifuls to telle I have no tome nowe,
Ne of his feynit fare that he fore with:
How goddes foght in the filde, folke as thai were! 45
And other errours unable, that after were knowen,
That poyetis of prise have prevyt untrew;
Ovyde and othir that onest were ay,
Virgille the virtuus, verrit for nobill,
Thes dampnet his dedys, and for dull holdyn. 50
   But the truth for to telle, and the text evyn,
Of that fight, how it felle in a few yeres,
That was clanly compilet with a clerke wise,
On Gydo, a gome that graidly hade soght,
And wist all the werkes by weghes he hade, 55
That bothe were in batell while the batell last,
And euther sawte and assembly see with there een.
Thai wrote all the werkes wroght at that tyme
In letturs of there langage, as thai lernede hade:
Dares and Dytes were duly there namys. 60
Dites full dere was dew to the Grekys,

---

36. *lympit of the sothe,* 'stumbled from the truth'

41. One of the medieval objections to Homer was no doubt his partisan support of the Greeks: Hector is the hero of the medieval Troy books.

45. The versions of Dares and Dictys excluded most of the Homeric supernatural. The medieval attitude to the classical gods was at best euhemeristic.

53–4. 'which was elegantly compiled by a wise clerk, one Guido, a man who had carefully researched, and knew all about the events from authors whom he had by him'

61. Dictys was the supposed companion of King Idomeneus of Crete in the Trojan War. There was a Greek account of it attributed to him, but whether or not this is represented by the fourth-century Latin prose work which bears his name is uncertain.

A lede of that lond, and logede hom with.
The tother was a tulke out of Troy selfe,
Dares, that duly the dedys behelde.
Aither brevyt in a boke on there best wise,   65
That sithen at a sité somyn were founden,
After, at Atthenes, as aunter befell.
The whiche bokes barely, bothe as thai were,
A Romayn overraght, and right hom hymselvyn,
That Cornelius was cald to his kynde nome.   70
He translated it into Latyn for lyking to here,
But he shope it so short that no shalke might
Have knowlage by course how the case felle;
For he brought it so breff, and so bare levyt,
That no lede might have likyng to loke therappon,   75
Til this Gydo it gate, as hym grace felle,
And declaret it more clere, and on clene wise.
    In this shall faithfully be founden, to the fer ende,
All the dedis bydene as thai done were:
How the groundes first grew, and the grete hate,   80
Bothe of torfer and tene that hom tide aftur,
And here fynde shall ye faire of the felle peopull:
What kynges ther come of costes aboute;
Of dukes full doughty, and of derffe erles,
That assemblid to the citie that sawte to defend;   85
Of the Grekys that were gedret, how gret was the nowmber,
How mony knightes there come, and kynges enarmede,
And what dukes thedur droghe for dedis of were;
What shippes there were shene, and shalkes within,
Bothe of barges and buernes that broght were fro Grese: 90
And all the batels on bent the buernes betwene;

---

64. Dares is mentioned by Homer as a Trojan priest of Hephaestus, and a
pre-Homeric Iliad was attributed to him in classical times. The Latin prose
De Excidio, which claims to be a translation of it, is a fifth-century compilation.

70. Cornelius Nepos, a Roman poet and historian, who lived during the
reign of Augustus. He was supposed to have found the works in an old cup-
board in Athens.

78ff. The poet sets out to give a complete factual record of the war in
Troy, and clearly sees his task as that of a chronicler.

What duke that was dede through dyntes of hond,
Who fallen was in fylde, and how it fore after.
Bothe of truse and of trayne the truth shalt thu here,
And all the ferlies that fell, unto the ferre ende.   95

Fro this prologue I passe, and part me therwith.
Frayne will I fer, and fraist of there werkes,
Meve to my mater, and make here an ende.

VII. Sir Thopas

Sir Thopas, Chaucer's burlesque metrical romance, gives the appearance of having been explicitly designed for the situation in which it is found in *The Canterbury Tales*. He is generally supposed to have started work on the *Tales* in about 1387, and may have gone on working at them until his death in 1400. However, some scholars consider that one of the main objects of the poem was to satirize the Flemish knighthood, in the person of the hero, and that it may have been written at the time of the Flemish embassy to London in 1383. There is no one model for *Sir Thopas*, but the poem is a patchwork of borrowings and echoes of many of the romances preserved in the Auchinleck MS which Chaucer seems to have known, and may have owned (see Introduction. p. 28). I print from the facsimile of the Ellesmere MS.

MS: Ellesmere 26.c.12, Huntington Library, California
Dialect: South-east Midlands, of London
Edition: The Complete Works of Geoffrey Chaucer, ed. F. N. Robinson, rev. edn
   (Cambridge, Mass., 1957)

(After the Prioress's affecting tale, the Host turns to Chaucer as a man likely to be able to amuse the company with a 'tale of myrth'. Chaucer knows only a rhyme that he learned long ago.)

> Listeth, lordes, in good entent,
> And I wol telle verrayment
>   Of myrthe and of solas;
> Al of a knyght was fair and gent
> In bataille and in tourneyment,
>   His name was Sire Thopas.
>
> Yborn he was in fer contree,
> In Flaundres, al biyonde the see,
>   At Poperyng, in the place.
> His fader was a man ful free,
> And lord he was of that contree,
>   As it was Goddes grace.

---

9. The men of Poperinghe, a town in Flanders, had a traditional reputation for stupidity.

Sir Thopas wax a doghty swayn;
Whit was his face as payndemayn,
   Hise lippes rede as rose;   15
His rode is lyk scarlet in grayn,
And I yow telle in good certeyn,
   He hadde a semely nose.

His heer, his berd, was lyk saffroun,
That to his girdel raughte adoun;   20
   His shoon of cordewane.
Of Brugges were his hosen broun,
His robe was of syklatoun,
   That coste many a jane.

He koude hunte a wilde deer,   25
And ride an haukyng for river
   With grey goshauk on honde;
Therto he was a good archeer;
Of wrastlyng was ther noon his peer,
   Ther any ram shal stonde.   30

Ful many a mayde, bright in bour,

---

14. *payndemayn*, 'fine white bread'. *Panis dominicus* may derive from the custom of stamping a figure of Christ or the Virgin on the loaf: more probably it denotes the superior bread served to the master or *dominus*.

16. *scarlet in greyn*—cloth dyed with cochineal.

20. The long beard had gone out of fashion by this time.

23. *syklatoun*, a costly cloth. The word is of Oriental origin, as is so often the case in medieval descriptions of luxury. The root is identical with that of 'scarlet' in Persian—originally denoting colour, by this time it refers to any costly, gold-embroidered material.

24. *jane*, a corruption of *Genoa*. A *jane* is a small Genoese coin. The Genoese were amongst the greatest trading peoples of the Middle Ages dealing particularly with the Orient.

26. *for river*, cf. IV. 68 for the verb *revey*, 'to hunt along the banks of a river'.

27. According to the manuals of hawking, the goshawk was a yeoman's bird.

28–30. Wrestling and archery, though not exclusive to the lower classes, were on the whole plebeian sports: Chaucer's Miller is a champion wrestler. The ram is the traditional prize for wrestling.

They moorne for hym paramour,
  Whan hem were bet to slepe;
But he was chaast and no lechour,
And sweete as is the brembul-flour   35
  That bereth the rede hepe.

And so bifel upon a day,
For sothe, as I yow telle may,
  Sir Thopas wolde out ride.
He worth upon his stede gray,
And in his hand a launcegay,   40
  A long swerd by his side.

He priketh thurgh a fair forest,
Therinne is many a wilde best—
  Ye, bothe bukke and hare;
And as he priketh North and Est,   45
I telle it yow, hym hadde almest
  Bitid a sory care.

Ther spryngen herbes grete and smale,
The lycorys and cetewale,
  And many a clowe-gylofre;   50
And notemuge to putte in ale,
Wheither it be moyste or stale,
  Or for to leye in cofre.

The briddes synge, it is no nay,
The sperhauk and the papejay,   55
  That joye it was to here;

---

39. *worth upon*, 'became upon', *i.e.* 'got on'.

40. *launcegay*, a kind of short lance. The word is a corruption of the Spanish *azagaya*, which denoted a dart or half-pike used by the Moors. It is of Moorish origin.

44. Typical of the deflationary method of the poem: compare the birds and plants with which the forest is stocked. The catalogues are a familiar feature of romance, but here they render the situation absurd by the details with which they are filled: it sounds more like a grocer's shop than a forest of romance.

The thrustelcok made eek hir lay,
The wodedowve upon the spray
    She sang ful loude and cleere.

    Sire Thopas fil in love-longynge,   60
Al whan he herde the thrustel synge,
    And pryked as he were woode.
His faire steede in his prykynge
So swatte that men myghte him wrynge;
    His sydes were al blood.   65

    Sire Thopas eek so wery was
For prikyng on the softe gras,
    So fiers was his corage,
That doun he leyde him in that plas
To make his steede som solas,   70
    And yaf hym good forage.

    'O Seinte Marie, *benedicite*!
What eyleth this love at me
    To bynde me so soore?
Me dremed al this nyght, pardee,   75
An elf-queene shal my lemman be
    And slepe under my goore.

    An elf-queene wol I love, ywis,
For in this world no womman is
    Worthy to be my make   80
        In towne;

61-2. The common association of 'love-longing' with the song of the birds
in the romances: *Guy of Warwick* is perhaps the most significant instance here.

66-71. A masterpiece of controlled inanity: every line a *non-sequitur*.

71. *forage*, probably another example of Thopas's knightly incompetence.
No knight in his senses would take dry fodder with him when his horse could
so obviously find grazing.

76. Love between a knight and a queen of faerie is a common situation,
especially in the Breton *lais*, but Sir Thopas's initiative in the affair, and his
presumption (79–81), are comic reversals of the tradition.

Alle othere wommen I forsake,
And to an elf-queene I me take
   By dale and eek by downe!'

Into his sadel he clam anon,   85
And priketh over stille and stoon
   An elf-queen for t'espye,
Til he so longe hath riden and goon
That he foond, in a privé woon,
   The contree of fairye   90
         So wilde;
For in that contree was ther noon
[That to him durste ride or goon,]
   Neither wyf ne childe;

Till that ther cam a greet geaunt,   95
His name was Sire Olifaunt,
   A perilous man of dede.
He seyde, 'Child, by Termagaunt!
But if thou prike out of myn haunt,
   Anon I sle thy steede   100
         With mace.
Heere is the queene of Fairye,
With harpe and pipe and symphonye,
   Dwellynge in this place.'

The child seyde, 'Also moote I thee,   105
Tomorwe wol I meete with thee,

93. Not in Ellesmere: supplied from Cambridge University MS
Dd.4.24

----

95. The giant guardian of the Fairy kingdom is a familiar feature of the
romances. He is often a herdsman, but here is 'Sir Elephant', a Saracen, to
judge by his oath 'by Termagaunt'.

101–2. The exploitation of the metre of the tail-rhyme romances for comic
purposes (cf. 90–1, 110–11). The 'tail' inevitably carries considerable emphasis,
but is here filled with embarrassingly superfluous detail.

103. *symphonye* is used in the Middle Ages of various kinds of musical
instruments; here, perhaps, a kind of tabor (Skeat).

Whan I have myn armoure;
And yet I hope, par ma fay,
That thou shalt, with this launcegay
   Abyen it full sowre.   110
       Thy mawe,
Thyn hauberk shal I percen, if I may,
Ere it be fully pryme of day,
   For heere thow shalt be slawe.'

Sire Thopas drow abak ful faste;   115
This geant at hym stones caste
   Out of a fel staf-slynge.
But faire escapeth Child Thopas,
And al it was thurgh Goddes gras,
   And thurgh his fair berynge.   120

Yet listeth, lordes, to my tale
Murier than the nightyngale;
   I wol yow rowne
How Sir Thopas, with sydes smale,
Prikyng over hill and dale,   125
   Is comen agayn to towne.

His murie men comanded he
To make hym bothe game and glee,
   For nedes moste he fighte
With a geaunt with hevedes three,   130
For paramour and jolitee
   Of oon that shoon ful brighte.

---

110. 'Thou shalt pay for it very bitterly'.

113. *pryme* is the period from 6 to 9 a.m. and *fully pryme* is thus 9 a.m.

117. *staf-slynge*, a sling attached to a stick to give extra power.

119–20. A conventional formula, though Thopas's escape seems due much rather to his own discretion.

124. *sydes smale*, a familiar formula, but one applied always to ladies.

130. The way in which this, the outstanding feature about the giant, is mentioned casually after Sir Oliphant has vanished from the scene, is a telling comment on the narrative ineptitude of the popular romances.

131. 'for the love and amusement of a lady'

'Do come,' he seyde, 'my mynstrales,
And geestours for to tellen tales,
   Anon in myn armynge,   135
Of romances that been roiales,
Of Popes and of cardinales,
   And eek of love-likynge.'

They fette hym first sweete wyn,
And mede eek in a mazelyn,   140
   And roial spicerye,
And gyngebreed that was ful fyn,
And lycorys, and eek comyn,
   With sugre that is so trye.

He dide next his white leere,   145
Of clooth of lake fyn and cleere,
   A breech and eek a sherte;
And next his sherte an aketoun,
And over that an haubergeoun,
   For percynge of his herte;   150

And over that a fyn hawberk,
Was al ywroght of Jewes werk,
   Ful strong it was of plate;
And over that his cote-armour,

---

133. '*Do come*' = 'summon'.

137. I imagine this is again satirical: one would not expect to find 'popes and cardinals' as heroes of romance.

145ff. It has been suggested that this account of Thopas's arming is part of the burlesque: that it again shows the bourgeois hopelessly at sea in the world of knighthood. It may be so, but there is a danger of pushing this interpretation too far. The startling omission is of any mention of his sword (though he has a sheath).

148–56. The *aketoun* is a quilted tunic, worn under the mail shirt: the *haubergeoun* is the coat of mail, and the *hawberk* seems here to refer to the back and breast plates worn over the chain-mail shirt, though this is an exceptional use of the term. There is evidence that the Jews were famous as armourers during the Middle Ages: certainly they were the principal dealers in armour and weapons.

As whit as is a lilye flour,   155
　In which he wol debate.

　His sheeld was al of gold so reed,
And therinne was a bores heed,
　A charbocle bisyde;
And there he swoor on ale and bread   160
How that the geaunt shal be deed,
　Bityde what bityde!

　His jambeux were of quyrboilly,
His swerdes shethe of yvory,
　His helm of latoun bright;   165
His sadel was of rewel boon,
His brydel as the sonne shoon,
　Or as the moone light.

　His spere was of fyn cipress,
That bodeth werre, and nothyng pees,   170
　The heed ful sharpe ygrounde;
His steede was al dappull gray,
It gooth an ambil in the way
　Ful softely and rounde
　　　In londe.   175
　Loo, lordes myne, heere is a fit!
If ye wol any moore of it,
　To telle it wol I fonde.

---

155. This may be a joke: the *cote-armour* should not have been blank, but should have carried the knight's armorial bearings.

160. Probably a parody of more dignified oaths in chivalric literature, *e.g.* by the peacock, the swan, the heron.

166. *rewel boon* is ivory made from whales' teeth. Probably the tusks of the walrus or narwhal.

169. The usual wood of the knight's spear was ash, so there may be some satirical point here. Cypress is traditionally associated with funerals, which may account for line 170, though one wonders whether the application is to Thopas or his opponent.

173. Hardly the pace one might expect of a war-horse.

Now holde youre mouth, *par charitee*
Both knyght and lady free   180
   And herkneth to my spelle;
Of batailles and of chivalry,
And of ladyes love-drury
   Anon I wol yow telle.

Men speken of romances of prys,   185
Of Horn Child and of Ypotys,
   Of Beves and of Sir Gy,
Of Sir Lybeux and Pleyndamour,
   But Sir Thopas, he bereth the flour
   Of roial chivalry!   190

His good steede al he bistrood,
And forth upon his way he rood
   As sparcle out of the bronde;
Upon his creest he bar a tour,
And therinne stiked a lilie flour,   195
   God shilde his cors from shonde!

And for he was a knyght auntrous,
He nolde slepen in noon house,
   But liggen in his hoode;
His brighte helm was his wonger,   200
And by hym baiteth his dextrer
   Of herbes fyne and goode.

---

179. A deliberate contrasting of an imagined aristocratic audience, and the manner of address to a popular one.

185ff. This kind of catalogue is a commonplace. The romances of *Beves of Hamtoun*, *Guy of Warwick*, and *Horn Child* all survive in the Auchinleck MS which Chaucer almost certainly knew (see Introduction, p. 28). *Libeus Desconus* is found in two late MSS with *Ypotys*. The latter is not a romance, and Chaucer may have been conscious of this, and using it satirically. There is no extant poem of *Pleyndamour*, though the name is to be found in Malory.

197–8. Presumably, as a knight-errant, he had taken a vow to do this.

Hymself drank water of the well,
As dide the knyght Sire Percyvell
So worthy under wede,   205
Til on a day—

(At this point the exasperated Host breaks in to stint Chaucer of his 'drasty rhyming'. He is to tell something in prose, and indeed he does, boring his modern audience this time to tears with the vast moral *Tale of Melibee*. The pilgrims, however, are satisfied.)

205. worthy: MS worly

203-4. This detail is preserved in the English poem of *Sir Perceval* which survives in the Thornton MS. Perceval too is a virgin and a fool—but a holy one.

VIII. Emaré

YET another version of a popular story, the 'Constance saga', *Emaré* was written in a form of the tail-rhyme stanza at about the turn of the fifteenth century. The story is also used at about this time by Gower in his *Confessio Amantis* (1390) and by Chaucer (*The Man of Law's Tale*). Both of these derive from the early fourteenth-century *Anglo-Norman Chronicle* of Nicholas Trivet. These versions take over something of the chronicle manner of their exemplar, and are told as moral tales, or even as hagiography. *Emaré*, however, is classed as a romance, and claims to be derived from a Breton *lai* (1030–2). The implications of this claim are discussed in the Introduction, pp. 37–8. No comparable French poem is extant, though the case for a French original is strong. There is no connexion with either Gower or Chaucer: the poem is the work of a rather mediocre popular entertainer.

Only one MS survives, of the mid-fifteenth century.

MS: British Museum MS Cotton Caligula A.ii
Dialect: Uncertain. North-east Midlands, of Yorkshire (Rickert), but Trounce would place it further south, near East Anglia.
Edition: The Romance of Emaré, ed. Edith Rickert, E.E.T.S., E.S. 99 (1908)

(Emaré is the daughter of an emperor, Sir Artyus, and his wife, Dame Erayne, who dies soon after the child is born. She is brought up by the lady, Abro, who educates her as the pattern of courtesy.)

(73)   The emperor of gentylle blode,
       Was a curteys lorde and a gode,
           In alle maner of thynge.
       Aftur, when hys wyf was dede,
       He ledde hys lyf yn weddewede,   5
           And myche loved playnge.
       Sone aftur, yn a whyle,

   5. He: MS And

---

6. *playnge:* probably sexual play. The emperor's lust is a vital factor in the plot, since he conceives an incestuous passion for Emaré.

7ff. This is the only version of the story in which this information occurs. *Cesyle* is Sicily, and it is interesting that in 1191, when Richard Coeur de Lion was in Sicily, King Tancred presented him with many rich gifts, including splendid cloths. Saracen weaving and embroidery from Sicily was famous throughout the period.

The ryche kynge of Cesyle
 To the emperour gan wende.
A ryche present wyth hym he browght,   10
A cloth that was wordylye wroght.
 He wellecomed hym as the hende.

Syr Tergaunte that nobylle knyght hyghte;
He presented the emperor ryght,
 And sette hym on hys kne,   15
Wyth that cloth rychyly dyght,
Fulle of stones ther hyt was pyght,
 As thykke as hyt myght be:
Off topaze and rubyes,
And othur stones of myche prys,   20
 That semely wer to se;
Of crapowtes and nakette,
As thykke ar they sette,
 For sothe, as Y say the.

The cloth was dysplayed sone,   25
The emperour lokede ther-upone,
 And myght hyt not se;
For glysteryng of the ryche ston
Redy syghte had he non,
 And sayde, 'How may thys be?'   30
The emperour sayde on hygh,

---

13. Rickert suggests that *Tergaunte* is a corruption of *Tancred*, but this is dubious. Tervagaunt, or Termagaunt is a common name for pagan heroes or gods in feudal poetry.

17ff. The catalogue of stones is a familiar feature of the romances: each stone possessed certain specific virtues: topaz, for example, kept water from boiling, cooled men's passions and killed toads. It is doubtful whether any precise lapidary significance attaches to the description here, though as the cloth should function as a love-charm, a careful author might have chosen his stones with this in mind.

22. *crapowtes:* the toadstone, which might be any of various stones, was fabled to be found in the head of a toad, and was valued as a powerful amulet. *nakette,* unidentified, is perhaps to be associated with *nacre,* mother-of-pearl.

'Sertes, thys ys a fayry,
    Or ellys a vanyte!'
The Kyng of Cysyle answered than,
'So ryche a jewelle ys ther non   35
    In alle Crystyante.'

The Amerayle dowghter of hethennes
Made thys cloth wythouten less,
    And wrowghte hyt alle wyth pride;
And purtreyed hyt wyth gret honour,   40
Wyth ryche golde and asowr,
    And stones on ylke a syde.
And, as the story telles in honde,
The stones that yn thys cloth stonde,
    Sowghte they wer fulle wyde.   45
Seven wynter hyt was yn makynge,
Or hyt was browghte to endynge,
    In herte ys not to hyde.

In that on korner made was
Ydoyne and Amadas,   50
    Wyth love that was so trewe;
For they loveden hem wyth honour,
Portrayed they wer wyth trewe-love-flour,
    Of stones bryght of hewe:
Wyth carbunkulle and safere,   55

---

35. jewelle: MS jwelle

32-3. 'Indeed, this is magic, or else some kind of illusion.' The cloth is in fact magic, but its function in the plot is sadly bungled.

37. See note, III. 154. The Emir's daughter is a common romance property.

46. Seven winters—the magic period for such tasks, cf. *Sir Gawain and the Green Knight*, 613.

50. *Ydoyne and Amadas*, the heroine and hero of one of the most popular medieval romances. There is no surviving English version of the story, but they are often referred to as patterns of true lovers, cf. IX. 486.

53. *trewe-love-flour*, Herb Paris. The setting of its four leaves resembles the true-love knot. The embroidery may contribute to the love-charm.

55. There does not appear to be any lapidary significance in this assortment of stones.

Kassydonys and onyx so clere,
　　Sette in golde newe;
Deamondes and rubyes,
And other stones of mychylle pryse
　　And menstrellys wyth her glewe.   60

In that othur corner was dyght
Trystram and Isowde so bryght,
　　That semely wer to se;
And for they loved hem ryght,
As fulle of stones ar they dyght,   65
　　As thykke as they may be:
Of topase and of rubyes,
And othur stones of myche pryse,
　　That semely wer to se;
Wyth crapawtes and nakette,   70
Thykke of stones ar they sette,
　　For sothe, as Y say the.

In the thrydde korner, wyth gret honour,
Was Florys and Dam Blawncheflour,
　　As love was hem betwene;   75
For they loved wyth honour,
Purtrayed they wer wyth trewe-love-flour,
　　Wyth stones bryght and shene:

60. glewe: MS gle

---

60. This may be a scribe's mistake, or simply an example of the flabby writing of the worst popular romances: the line is a complete non-sequitur.

62. The story of Tristram and Iseult was one of the most influential of the romances from the twelfth century onwards, particularly as exemplifying passionate love. It probably owes inclusion here to the French source, although the forms of the names are English.

65-72. cf. 17-24. Almost exact duplication. It may, of course, be a scribal mistake, but the whole tissue of the poem is so feebly repetitious that it is probably original. Note the unintelligent repetition of the pattern in the four stanzas describing the cloth, and compare the much more accomplished description of Myldore's chamber in IX, which is in very similar vein.

74. See the Introduction to III, p. 76.

Ther wer knyghtus and senatowres,
Emerawdes of gret vertues,   80
        To wyte wythouten wene;
Deamoundes and koralle,
Perydotes and crystalle,
        And gode garnettes bytwene.

In the fourthe korner was oon,   85
Of Babylone the Sowdan sonne,
        The Amerayles dowghtyr hym by.
For hys sake the cloth was wrowght;
She loved hym in hert and thowght,
        As testymoyeth thys storye.   90
The fayr mayden her byforn
Was portrayed an unykorn,
        Wyth hys horn so hye;
Flowres and bryddes on ylke a syde,
Wyth stones that wer sowghte wyde,   95
        Stuffed wyth ymagerye.

(After the King of Sicily departs, the emperor sends for his daughter. He
falls in love with her, and determines to marry her. When she refuses, he casts
her adrift in a small boat, but repents as soon as she is gone. Emaré drifts
ashore in Galys, where she is received by a knight called Sir Kador. She comes
to the notice of the King, who falls in love with her and marries her. His
mother, however, takes her to be a fiend, and when the king is away at war,
persuades him in a letter that Emaré has given birth to a monster. Although the
king orders that nothing shall be done until he returns, the old queen intercepts
his letter, and has Emaré and the child cast adrift once more.)

---

79. It is just possible that these are a superior kind of emerald, but more
likely the line is produced by the same kind of sleepwalking as produced line 60.
86. There are two surviving English romances figuring the 'Sowdan of
Babylon', one so entitled, and *Sir Ferumbras*. He is a familiar figure in the
chansons de geste.
90. *testymoyeth*, 'testifies'. Probably influenced by the French *tesmoigner* in
the translator's original.
91. 'before the fair maiden'
92. The unicorn could only be caught and tamed by a virgin.
96. Sicilian work was in fact embroidered and decorated in this way
(Rickert).

(649) The lady and the lytylle chylde
       Fleted forth on the water wylde,
           Wyth fulle harde happes.
       Her surkote that was large and wyde,   100
       Therwyth her vysage she gan hyde,
           Wyth the hynther lappes;
       She was aferde of the see,
       And layde her gruf upon a tre,
           The chylde to her pappes.   105
       The wawes, that were grete and strong,
       On the bote faste they thonge,
           Wyth mony unsemely rappes.

       And when the chyld gan to wepe,
       Wyth sory herte she songe hyt aslepe,   110
           And putte the pappe yn hys mowth,
       And sayde, 'Myght Y onus gete lond,
       Of the watur that ys so stronge,
           By northe or by sowthe,
       Wel owth Y to warye the, see,   115
       I have myche shame yn the!'
           And ever she lay and growht.
       Then she made her prayer,
       To Jhesu and hys moder dere,
           In alle that she kowthe.   120

       Now thys lady dwelled there
       A fulle sevene nyght and more,
           As hyt was Goddys wylle;
       Wyth karefulle herte and sykyng sore,

       112. Myght: MS Myghth

   100-2. This detail is peculiar to *Emaré*, and suggests that at the time when
the poem was written, long surcoats were unfamiliar.
   104. 'and lay face-down across a thwart'
   109. In this scene of pathos, Emaré reaches as much artistic success as it ever
has. Gower's account at this point is rather similar, though unrelated.
   112-13. 'If only I could make land, out of this rough sea!'
   117. *growht* apparently a preterite form of *grucchen*, 'complain'.

Such sorow was her yarked yore,   125
    And she lay fulle stylle.
She was dryven toward Rome,
Thorow the grace of God yn trone,
    That alle thyng may fulfylle.
On the see she was so harde bestadde,   130
For hungur and thurste allemost madde,
    Wo worth chawnses ylle!

A marchaunte dwelled yn that cyté,
A ryche mon of golde and fee,
    Jurdan was hys name.   135
Every day wolde he
Go to playe hym by the see,
    The eyer for to tane.
He wente forth yn that tyde,
Walkynge by the see sythe,   140
    Alle hymself alone.
A bote he fonde by the brymme,
And a fayr lady therynne,
    That was ryght wo-by-gone.

The cloth on her shon so bryht,   145
He was aferde of that syght,
    For glysteryng of that wede;
And yn hys herte he thowght ryght,
That she was non erdyly wyght,

128. of: MS yf
133. dwelled: MS is damaged here, and *el* supplied
136. Every: MS Eevery
145. bryht: MS bryth
148 thowght: MS thowghth

---

135. In the versions of the story where the heroine arrives at Rome, the rescuer is usually a senator or a cardinal, sometimes the Pope.

142. *by the brymme* could mean 'by the shore' or 'by the sea'—probably the second.

146ff. This is the main unifying motif of the poem.

He sawe nevur non such yn leede.   150
He sayde, 'What hette ye, fayr ladye?'
'Lord,' she sayde, 'Y hette Egarye,
    That lye her yn drede."
Up he toke that fayre ladye,
And the yonge chylde her by,   155
    And hom he gan hem lede.

(Emaré and her son live happily at Rome for many years. Meanwhile, her husband having returned home from the wars and discovered what has happened, lives in grief. At last he decides to go to Rome for penance, where he is reunited to his wife by means of the child. The emperor too repents, and is finally reconciled with his daughter.)

150 such: MS shuch

---

152. *Egarye* is the name which Emaré first adopts when cast up in Galys. It is from the French *esgarée* and means 'outcast'. The lay which the English poem claims to represent is the *playn the garye*, i.e. *Playnt d'Egarye. Emaré* may be identified with the *Blonde Esmerée* of *Li Biaus Desconneus*, i.e. 'pure, refined as gold, rare', etc.

IX. Sir Degrevant

THIS romance, probably written at the turn of the fifteenth century in a sixteen-line tail-rhyme stanza, survives in two MSS of the mid-century, one of which is the famous Thornton MS. Another poem in this MS, *Sir Percyvelle of Galles*, also illustrates this unusual stanza-form. No one source for the poem can be adduced: it appears to be a composite of stock incidents from several poems. The roughly contemporary *Erle of Toulous* in particular, and the alliterative *Morte Arthure*, offer certain parallels: it is perhaps significant that both are found in the Thornton MS. I do not, however, print from this (Lincoln Cathedral MS A.5.2), but from the Cambridge version, which is slightly later, but preserves a more accurate text.

MS: Cambridge University Library MS Ff.i.6
Dialect: North-east, with northern admixture. There is some internal evidence, however, for East Anglian origin and the Cambridge copy seems to have been made to the south-west of the area of composition.
Edition: Sir Degrevant, ed. L. F. Casson, E.E.T.S., O.S. 221 (1944)
Text: I have preserved a number of scribal peculiarities, notably the doubling of consonants. Final spellings like -ghth are regularized to -ht.

(1)	Lord Gode in Trynite,	
	Yeff home hevene for to se	
	That lovethe gamen and gle,	
	And gestus to fede.	
	Ther folke sitis in fere	5
	Shullde men herken and here	
	Off gode that before [hem] were	
	That levede in arthede.	
	And Y schall karppe off a knyght	
	That was both hardy and wyght:	10

2. for: MS ffor. Initial *ff* is simplified throughout

1ff. The conventional opening of the tail-rhyme romances: the professional entertainer's bid for a hospitable reception.

8. *arthede*, 'people (nation) of long ago': a rare word. Either from OE *ærtheod* with Scandinavian influence to *ar-* or OE *ærgetheod*.

Sir Degrevaunt that hend hyght,
 That dowghty was of dede;
Was never knyght that he fond,
In Fraunce ne in Englond,
Myght sette a schafft of hys hond   15
 On a stythe stede.

Wyth Kyng Arrtor, Y wene,
And wyth Gwennor the quene,
He was known for kene,
 That comelych knyght,   20
In Hethenesse and in Spayne,
In Fraunce and in Bryttayne,
Wyth Persevall and Gawayne,
 For hardy and wyght.
He was dowghty and der,   25
And ther nevew full ner,
Ther he of dedys myght yher
 By days or by nyght;
Forthy they name hem that stounde
A knyght of Tabull Round   30
As maked is in the mappe-mound,
 In storye full ryght.

13. knyght: MS kyngh

---

11. *Degrevaunt.* Perhaps the hero is identical with *Agravayn a la dure mayn*, a familiar name in Arthurian romance, who was son of King Lot of Lothian and nephew to Arthur (26). In French romances, the name sometimes appeared as *d'Egrivaunt* or *d'Egrivauns* and this kind of misreading by English translators is not unknown. However, there is no record of any French romance which had Agravayn as its hero, and the Arthurian connexion here is only nominal.

21. Degrevant's exploits are historically possible: this is symptomatic of the generally naturalistic intention of the poet.

25-6. There appears to be textual corruption: a simple transposition of these lines would improve the sense.

29-32. *the mappe-mound.* Perhaps there is a reference to some kind of chart or list of Arthur's knights. The 'Round Table' preserved at Winchester had such a chart, and Henry III had a *mappa mundi* painted in the same hall. But perhaps the term means no more than 'the world' itself: 'They elected him, therefore, to be a Knight of the Round Table, as is written in story in the world' (Casson).

He was fayre man and free,
And gretlech yaff hym to gle:
To harp and to sautre,   35
    And geterne full gay;
Well to play on a rote,
Off lewtyng, well Y wote,
And syngyng many seyt not,
  He bar the pryes aey.   40
Yet gamenes hade he mare:
Grehondes for hert and hare,
Both for bokes and the bare,
    By nyght and be day;
Fell faukons and fayr,   45
Haukes off nobull eyre,
Tyll his parke ganne repeyr,
    By sexxty, Y dar say.

He wold be upp or the day
To honte and to revay;   50
Gretly yaff hem to pley
    Eche day to newe;
To here hys mas or he went
Trewly in gode entaunt,
And sethe to bowe into the bente   55
    There games ine grewe.
Now to forest he founde,
Both wyth horne and with hound;
To breyng the deere to the ground
    Was hys most glew.   60

37. on: MS in
50. and to: MS to and to
58. wyth: MS wyt

33ff. The hero is a skilful minstrel, and honours his brother artists. The list of accomplishments is conventional, but much more sophisticated than, say, Havelok's.

37. *rote*, a lyre-shaped instrument, played like a harp.

50. *revay*, 'hunt or hawk along the river-bank', cf. IV. 68.

Certus, wyff wold he non,
Wench ne lemon,
But as an anker in a ston
    He lyved ever trew.

Ther was sesyd in hys hand   65
A thousand poundus worth off land
Off rentes well settand,
    And muchell dell more;
An houndered plows in demaynus,
Fayer parkes in-wyth haynus,   70
Grett herdus in the playnus,
    Wyth muchell tame store;
Castelos wyth heygh wallus,
Chambors wyth noble hallus,
Fayer stedes in the stallus,   75
    Lyard and soore.
Wher he herd of anny cry,
Ever he was redy;
He passede never forth by
    In londe wher they were.   80

He lovede well almosdede,
Powr men to cloth and fede
Wyth menske and manhede;
    Off met he was fre.

68. muchell: MS muchll

---

63. 'like a hermit in a cell'. The combination of generosity in alms-giving, valour in war and diffidence in love is a frequent one among knightly heroes. In fact, though, Degrevant is not a notably diffident lover.

65ff. The solidity of the social, economic and topographical setting in this poem is remarkable: one does not normally expect to be informed of a romance hero's sources of income.

69ff. The poet shows considerable technical knowledge concerning property and forest law. Demesne land (*demaynus*) is land held in one's own right, not as a tenant. A park was land enclosed by a fence or paling, to keep your deer in or your neighbours' deer out. A warren was unenclosed land, over which one had hunting rights over beasts *ferae naturae* (Casson).

77. *cry* here apparently 'an appeal for justice, a complaint'.

And also gestes to call   85
And mensteralus her in halle,
He yaff hem robes off palle,
    Off gold and off fee.
In ych place whaer he come,
When he went fram hem,   90
They hade halowed hys name
    Wyth gret nobulle.
In ych lond wher he wentt
So many men he hadde schentt,
In justus and on tornament   95
    He whan ever the gre.

Ther wonede an eorl him besyd,
Ye, a lord off mechell pryd,
That hadd viij forestes ful wyd,
    And bowres full brode.   100
He hade a grete spyt of the knyght
That was so hardy and wyght,
And thought howe he best myght
    That dowghty to grade.
He was sterne and stoute,   105
And rode in a gay route,
And brak hys parkes about,
    The best that he hade;
Therinne he made a sory pley,
The fattest he feld, in fey,   110
By sexty on a day,
    Suche maystries he made.

He drowhe reveres with fysh,
And slogh hys forsteres, ywys:

104. grade: MS grde

85–8. We are reminded on several occasions of Degrevant's generosity to minstrels: these were the usual gifts anticipated.

96. 'He always carried off the prize.'

110. *i.e.* the fattest deer.

The knyght wyste not of thys,   115
    For soth Y you say,
For he was in the Holy Lond,
Dede of armes for to fond;
The hethene men wyth hys hond
    He feld hem offten in fey.   120
Hys steward hadd a lettre ysent,
A mesynger hath hyt hent,
And forth hys wey ys ywent
    As fast as ever he mey.
When he tyll hys lord com,   125
The lettre in hys hand he nom;
He sey all yoode to schom,
    And went on hys wey.

Wyth the knytht was non abad,
He buskyd hym forth and rade   130
Fram the frount of Garnad
    As faste as he myght.
Sone he pased the see,
He and hys meney,
And com into hys contre   135
    By the twelthe nyght.
Tyll hys manere he went,
A feyr place he fond schent,
Hys housbondus that yaf rent
    Was yheryghed doun ryght.   140

    131. Garnad: MS the Garnad

117–20. Although Sir Degrevant's adventures are historically and politically probable, he fights for personal and chivalrous reasons, undertaking 'deeds of arms' for his own renown.

127. sey: Casson emends to seyde, 'said', and makes the messenger the subject. If Degrevant were the subject, however, which is arguable, sey could be a preterite form of see: 'He saw that everything was going to rack and ruin.'

131. Garnad, 'Granada'. Degrevant had fought in Spain as well as the Holy Land, though we are not told how he got from one to the other. frount is used in its military sense.

137. Similar passages occur in other English romances, e.g. The Tale of Gamelyn. The Erle of Toulous has a similar situation but lacks the detail.

His tenantrie was all doun,
The best in every toun,
His fayr parkes wer comoun,
      And lothlych bydyght.

He closed hys parkes ayen—   145
His husbondus they were fyen—
He lent hem oxon and wayn
      Of his own store;
And also sede for [to] sowe,
Wyght horse for to draw,   150
And thought werke be lawe
      And wyth non other schore.
Forthi a lettre had he dyght
To this eorl opo myght:
He preyd hem to do him ryght   155
      Ar tell hym wherfore;
And wyth sqwer he hit sent
Off an honderd pond of rent,
And forth hys wey ys he went
      To wytt hys answer.   160

The squier nolde nat down lyght,
Bot haylis this eorl opon hyght,
And sethes barown and knyght
      With wordes full wise;
He held the lettre by the nooke   165
And to the eorle he hit toke,

143. comoun: MS comen
163. barown: MS bowron

---

141. *tenantrie*, 'tenants' holdings, houses'.

145ff. Note that the hero's first actions are those of a careful landlord, not of a chivalric hero. And he tries at first to obtain redress by legal means, not force.

146. 'his tenants were glad of that'

158. 'with an income of a hundred pounds a yea'r. A curious detail.

160-1. There is a stanza missing here in the Cambridge MS. According to the Thornton MS the squire meets the earl and his men in the act of trespass.

And he thereon gan loke
 And seyde his avys;
And spake to the squiere:
'Ne were thou a messengere,   170
Thou shuld abey ryght here
 Under this wode-rys!
I wull, for thy lordes tene,
Honte hys forestus and grene,
And breke his parkes bydene,   175
 Proudeste of prys.'

Thanne the squier seyde sone:
'Syre, that is nat well done!
Ye have lefft hym bote whone,
 In herte is nat to hyde.   180
He that seyth that hit is ryght,
Be he squier other knyght,
Here my glove on to fyght,
 What chaunce so betyde!
Syr, yeff hit be your well,   185
Thenkes that ye han don ylle;
Y rede ye amend to schkyll,
 For wothes is ever wyde.'
The eorl answeryd, 'Ywyse,
Y woll nat amend that mese.   190
Y counte hym nat at a cres,
 For all hys mechell pryd.'

Than the eorl wax wroth
And swor many a gret owth,
He schold be messaggere lothe   195

193. wroth: MS wth

---

179. 'You have left him only one remedy' (*i.e.* force).
188. *wothes* = OE *wath*, 'wandering, roving, hunting'. Perhaps, then: 'for your extensive ravages'.
191. 'I reckon him at the worth of a cress', *i.e.* something of no account.
195–6. 'Unless he went away, he would regret ever having brought such a message.'

But he hys wey wente.
He toke his leve withouten nay,
And wendus forth on his way
As fast as ever he may
    Over the brode bent.   200
He com hom at the none,
And told how he hade done;
The knyght asked him as sone
    What answer he sent.
'Sir, and he may as he ment,   205
His game woll he never stent.
Thyself, and he may the hent,
    I tell the for yschent.'

Than Syr Degrevaunt syght,
And byheld the heven upan hyght: 210
'Jhesu, save me in my ryght,
    And Maré me spede!
And Y schall yeff Gode a vow:
Som of us schall hyt rew;
Hyt schall not be for his prow,   215
    And Y may right rede.'
Anon to armus they hom dyght,
As fast as ever they myght,
Both squier and knyght,
    Wys under wede;   220
Ther was y-armed on hye
Ten score knythis redy,
And iij hondred archerus by,
    Full goode at her nede.

Anon to the forest they found,   225
Ther they stotede a stound,

205–8. 'If he has his way, he will never leave off his tricks—and if he can catch you, you'll be a dead man, I reckon.'

221ff. The battle is a composite of many traditional formulae, but the substance and arrangement may owe something to the battle in *The Erle of Toulous* between the hero and the emperor.

They pyght pavelouns round,
 And loggede that nyght.
The eorl purveyede him an ost,
And com in at anothur cost   230
Wyth his brag and his bost,
 Wyth many a ferres knyght.
He uncouplede his houndus
Withinne the knyghtus boundus,
Bothe the grene and the groundus   235
 They halowede an hyght.
Thus the forest they fray,
Hertus bade at abey;
On a launde by a ley
 These lordus doune lyght.   240

Sexten hertus wase yslayn
And wer brought to a pleyn,
Byfore the cheff cheventen
 Yleyd wer yfere.
Thane seys the [eorl] on the land: 245
'Wher ys now Sir Degrevaund?
Why wol not com this gyant
 To rescow his dere?
Hys proud hertes of grese
Bereth no chartur of pes;   250
We schall have som ar we sese—
 Y wolde he wer here.
Trewely, ar he went,
He schuld the game repent,
The proud lettre that he sent   255
 By his sqwer.'

248. rescow: MS recow

---

235. There is no real distinction here: 'grounds' includes the whole of the knight's land and 'green' simply denotes the grassy parts of it.
249–50. 'His proud, fat harts carry no peace-treaty with them' (perhaps, 'have no safe-conduct').

Syr Degrevaunt was so nere
That he the wordes can her.
He seyd, 'Avaunt baner,
       And trompes apon hyght!'   260
Hys archarus that wer thare,
Both lase and the mar,
As swythe wer they thare,
       To shote wer they dyght.
Thane the eorle was payd,   265
Sone his batell was reyde,
He was no-thyng afreyd
       Off that feris knyght.
Now ar they met on a feld
Both with spere and sheld,   270
Wyghtly wepenes they weld,
       And ferysly they fyght.

And whan the batell ennjoined,
With speres ferisly they foynede:
Ther no sege be ensoynd   275
       That faught in the feld.
Wyth bryght swerdus on the bent
Rych hawberkes they rent,
Gleves, gleteryng glent
       Opon geldene scheldus.   280
They styken stedus in stour,
Knyghtus thorow her armere;
Lordus off honor

261–4. An illustration of contemporary tactics: this is not the usual stylized encounter of the chivalric romance.

267–8. This is inconsistent with the later picture of the earl shirking a direct encounter with Sir Degrevant: he may, of course, have been overawed by the hero's prowess in this fight.

277ff. Note that in the battle-descriptions the proportion of alliterative phrases increases remarkably: many of them are formulae found in Old English heroic poetry.

> Opon the hethe heldus.
> They foughten so ferisly   285
> Ther weste non so myghty
> Who schold have the victory,
>   Bot He that all weldus.

> The doughty knyght Sur Degrevant
> Leys the lordes on the laund   290
> Thorw jepun and jesseraund,
>   And lames the ledes.
> Schyr scheldus they schrede,
> Many dowghty was dede,
> Ryche maylus wexen rede,   295
>   So manye bolde dedus.
> Thus they fowghten on frythe,
> Kene knyghtus inwith kith,
> Wo wrekes thare wryth
>   These doughty on dede!   300
> Burnes he hadde yborn doun,
> Gomes wyth gambisoun
> Lyes opon bent broun,
>   And sterff under stede.

> Sir Degrevaunt the gode knyght   305
> Bryttenes the basnettus bryght;
> Hys feris ferysly they fyght

284. hethe: MS heth^ene
285. They: MS Then
298. knyghtus: MS kynghus
306 Bryttenes: MS Brghtenes

---

284. I accept Casson's emendation *hethe*, 'heath, moor', with some reluctance. The MS reading *heth(e)ne* does make (unlikely) sense: 'fall upon the heathen'. It sometimes happens that Christian villains are turned into unbelievers by an excited poet.

285-8. 'They fought so fiercely that no-one, however powerful, except God alone the ruler of all, might know who should win.'

291. *jesseraund*, a coat of mail made of small riveted plates.

302. *gambisoun*, a leather tunic, worn by foot-soldiers, protecting the trunk and thighs.

And felles hom to grond.
The knyghtus of the eorlus hous
That were yhalden so chyvalerus   310
And in batell so bountyveus,
    They deyden all that stond.
The eorl hovede and beheld,
Both with sper and with scheld
How they fayr in the feld,   315
    And syght unsound.
The best men that he ledde
He had ylefft hom to wedde;
With fyffty spers is he gledd,
    And wodelech was ywounded.   320

Syr Degrivant and his men
Felde hom faste in the fen,
As the deer in the den
    To dethe he tham denges.
Wyth scharpe axus of stell   325
He playtede her basnetus well;
Many a knyght gart he knell
    In the mornyng.
Sir Degrevant was full thro,
Departed her batell atwo,   330
The eorl fley and was wo,
    On a stede can he spryng.
He laf slaw in a slak
Forty scor on a pak,
Wyd open on her bake,   335
    Dede in the lyng.

Syr Degrevant gat a sted
That was gode in ilk a ned,

327. knyght, MS knygh

---

310. *chyvalerus* seems to denote here only military prowess. The word is
rare in the poem.
317-18. 'He had left his best men as a pledge' (*i.e.* dead on the field).

Many a side gart he bled
    Thorow dent of his spere,   340
And schased the eorl within a whyll
More then enleve mylle.
Many bold gert he syle,
    That byfore dud hym dere.
He com schygynge ayen,   345
And of hys folk was fyen,
And fond never on slayn,
    Ne worse be a pere.
He knelede doun in that place
And thankyd God of His grace: 350

    Tyll his feyr manere.

Bleve to soper they dyght,
Both squier and knyght;
They daunsed and revelide that nyght,   355
    In hert wer they blythe.
And whan the eorl com ham
He was wonded to scham;
The lady ses he was lam,
    And swouned full swyth.   360
Offte she cryed, 'Alas!
Have ye nat parkus and chas?
What schuld ye do at is place,
    Swych costus to kythe?'
'Dame,' he seys, 'Y was thare,   365

345 schygynge: MS schgynge
354. knyght: MS knygh

---

345. *schygynge*. I follow Casson's emendation. The word appears to be
related to the more familiar forms 'shog' and 'jog': the sense here is something
like 'trotting'.

348. 'nor worse by a pear' (*i.e.* not a bit the worse).

350–1. A line is clearly missing in the MS.

362. *chas*, 'chase'—unenclosed land, kept for hunting.

364. Apparently 'to behave like this', but 'to receive such treatment' would
be nearer the sense.

And me rews now full sar.
I take m[y leve] for evermare
　　　Swych wronges to wrythe.'

(On going to the Earl's castle to renew his challenge, Degrevant sees his
enemy's daughter, Myldore, and falls in love. As hostilities continue, he has
difficulty in making his feelings known, but through the agency of his squire
and Myldore's maid, a meeting takes place, though Myldore will not commit
herself to love. The Earl has arranged a tournament, at which the Duke of
Gerle is to joust for Myldore's hand. Degrevant enters the lists and defeats the
Duke in three successive encounters. Struck by the hero's prowess and appearance, Myldore acknowledges her feeling for him, and a secret meeting at night
in her chamber is arranged.)

(1377)　The lady of honowre
　　　Metes the [knyght] in the doure,　　　　　　　370
　　　Knelyd doun in the floure,
　　　　　And fel hym to feet.
　　　Frek as fuyre in the flynt,
　　　He in armes had hyr hynt,
　　　And thritty sythes, ar he stynt,　　　　　　　375
　　　　　He kyst that swet.
　　　'Welcome, Sure Aunterous,
　　　Me thenkus thou art mervelous;
　　　Wyst my lord of this hous,
　　　　　Wyth grame would the gret.'　　　　　　　380
　　　Swythe chayres was isette,
　　　And quyschonus of vyolete;
　　　Thus this semely was isete
　　　　　With mouth for to mete.

　　　'Damisele, loke ther be　　　　　　　　　　385

367. m(y leve): MS is damaged: supplied from Thornton
368. wronges: MS wornges

367–8. This does not make the sense the context requires. The earl surely
means 'I won't do it again'; he *says*, 'I forgo for ever the opportunity of
righting such wrongs.'
369–72. A reversal of the roles of lover and mistress in the romances of
courtly love.

A fuyre in the chymene,
Fagattus of fyre-tre.'
    That fecchyd was yare.
Sche sett a bourd of yvore,
Trestellus ordeyned therfor—   390
Clothus keverede that ovur,
    Swyche seye thei never are.
Towellus of Eylyssham,
Whyght as the seeys fame,
Sanappus of the same,   395
    Thus servyd thei ware.
With a gyld saler,
Basyn and ewer,
Watyr of euerrose clere,
    They wesche ryght there.   400

Paynemayn privayly
Sche brought fram the pantry,
And served that semely
    Same ther thei seet.

388. fecchyd: MS fetthyd
394. Whyght: MS Whyghth
400. ryght: MS ryghth
402. brought: MS broughth

389ff. The details in this passage, the ivory table-top, the trestles to support it, the table-cloth, may be paralleled in French and German romances. See also *Sir Gawain and the Green Knight*, 875–7, etc.

393. *Eylyssham*, the modern Aylsham, in Norfolk, about 14 miles north of Norwich. In the fourteenth century it was the chief linen town in the country. Scholars have been tempted to take this detail as localizing the poem in East Anglia, but if the town was nationally famous, this diminishes the force of the argument.

399. *euerrose:* rose-water was often used in the medieval toilet.

401. *Paynemayn*, see note on VII. 14.

401ff. The description of feasting is one of the stock means of heightening the luxurious atmosphere of romance. The account here is relatively moderate, though sumptuous: the menu is not exotic in its constituents. The situation, with the meal being served in the lady's chamber, rather than in the great hall, is comparatively rare, though parallels exist.

Sche brought fram the kychene   405
A scheld of a wylde swyne,
Hastelettus in galantyne,
    An hand Y yow hete.
Sethe sche brought hom in haste
Ploverys poudryd in paste—   410
Ther ware metus with the maste,
    I do yow to wytte.
Fatt conyngus and newe,
Fesauntus and corelewe,
Ryche she tham drewe   415
    Vernage and crete.

To tell here metus was ter
That was served at her soper;
Ther was no dentethus to dere,
    Ne spyces to spare.   420
And evere sche drow hom the wyn,
Bothe the roche and the reyn,
And the good malvesyn
    Felde sche hom yare.
And evere Myldore sche sete   425
Harpyng notus ful swet,
And otherwhyle sche et
    Whan hur leveste ware.
Songe yeddyngus above,
Swyche murthus they move;   430
In the chaumbur of love
    Thus thei sleye care.

430. Swyche: MS Sw che—the letter is illegible

---

406. cf. *The Master of Game:* 'Thei (*i.e.* boars) have herde skynne and stronge flessh, and specially upon the shoulder, that is called the shelde.' It does not sound much of a delicacy, but apparently the tough skin was used as a kind of case in which more tender meat was cooked.

431. The lady's bower is obviously appropriate for love-making, but *the chaumbur of love* is not in the same verbal category as 'the dining-room'. For a discussion of this passage see Introduction, pp. 39–40

Ther was a ryal rooffe
In the chaumbur of loffe;
Hyt was buskyd above   435
    With besauntus ful bryght.
All off ruel-bon,
Whyght ogee and parpon,
Mony a dereworthe stone
    Endentyd and dyght.   440
Ther men myght se, ho that wolde,
Arcangelus of rede golde,
Fyfty mad of o molde,
    Lowynge ful lyght;
With the Pocalyps of Jon,   445
The Powlus Pystolus everychon,
The Parabolus of Salamon
    Payntyd ful ryght.

And the foure Gospellorus
Syttyng on pyllorus;   450
Hend, herkeneth and herus,
    Gyf hyt be youre wyll.
Austin and Gregory,
Jerome and Ambrose,
Thus the foure doctorus   455
    Lystened than tylle.

    438. ogee: MS oger

---

437. *ruel-bon*, cf. VII. 166 note

438. I accept Casson's emendation. *Ogee* and *parpon* as architectural terms
would only recently have come into English use when this poem was written.

443. 'fifty, each after the same design'. 'The author is probably referring to
stone corbels, carved in the form of archangels and then gilded. In a church
of the period, the corbels might be set at the end of vertical shafts dividing the
spandrels of the arches and helping to support the roof. The description is a
clear suggestion of the frozen glories of the Perpendicular style' (Casson).
One might also adduce the great wooden hammer-beam roofs of East Anglian
churches such as March: the angels appear not only below the corbels, but also
on the ends of the hammers and on the middle of the collars. Such roofs
mostly date from the early fifteenth century.

447. *i.e.* The Book of Proverbs.

There was purtred in ston
The fylesoferus everychon,
The story of Absolon
    That lyked ful ylle;   460
With an orrelegge on hyght,
To rynge the ours at nyght,
To waken Myldore the bryght
    With bellus to knylle.

Square wyndowus of glas,   465
The rechest that ever was,
Tho moynelus was off bras,
    Made with menne handus;
Alle the wallus of geete,
With gaye gablettus and grete,   470
Kynggus syttyng in ther sete,
    Out of sere londus:
Grete Charlus with the croune,
Syre Godfray de Boyloune,

463. the bryght: MS t ryghth—two letters illegible
465. glas: MS gl s—letter illegible
470. sere: MS s re
474. de: MS the

460. Casson emends to *layked*, 'played, behaved'. But as it stands, the line has some meaning—'who pleased (everyone) very ill, who was very unsatisfactory'.

461. Many of the most elaborately sophisticated French romances include a long description of some mechanical toy. From this point on, the description tallies more closely with those of interiors in French romance, which are wholly secular. Casson remarks that a painted chamber discovered about twenty years ago in Longthorpe Hall near Peterborough combines in its early fourteenth-century murals sacred, didactic and secular subjects as this does. The East Midlands location is interesting.

465. Glazed windows were a sign of luxury, even as late as the end of the fourteenth century, and are often included as a heightening detail in romances of the period.

471. The kings appear to be the Nine Worthies, 'three Paynims, three Jews, and three Christian men'. Only the Christians are here named. Lists of the Worthies figure in two of the poems considered to have influenced *Sir Degrevant*, *Les Voeux du Paon* and the alliterative *Morte Arthure*.

And Arthur the Bretoune,   475
    With here bryght brondus.
The flour was paved overal
With a clere crystal,
And over-keveryd with a pal,
    A flore where she stondes.   480

Hur bed was off aszure
With testur and celure,
With a bryght bordure,
    Compasyd ful clene.
And all a storye as hyt was   485
Of Ydoyne and Amadas,
Perreye in ylke a plas,
    And papageyes of grene.
The scochenus of many knyght
Of gold and cyprus was idyght,   490
Brode besauntus and bryght,
    And trewelovus bytwene.
Ther was at hur testere
The kyngus owun banere;
Was never bede rychere   495
    Of empryce ne qwene.

Fayr schetus of sylk,
Chalk-whyght as the mylk,
Quyltus poyned of that ylk,
    Touseled they ware.   500

485-6. This is more in keeping with the atmosphere of sensuality which the situation would seem to require. See notes on VIII. 5off.

487-92. Popinjays (parrots) and *trewelovus* are associated in the description of the embroidered covering for the hero's helmet in *Sir Gawain and the Green Knight* (611-12)

500. Casson suggests that *touseled* is a dialect form of *tasseled*, referring to the quilts. This seems likely, though I am tempted by the modern meaning of *tousled*, 'rumpled'. Though out of keeping with the formal elegance of the description as a whole, rumpled bedclothes would inject some much-needed sensual excitement into the scene.

Coddys of sendal,
Knoppus of crystal
That was mad in West-fal
    With women of lare.
Hyt was a mervelous thing   505
To se the rydalus hyng
With mony a rede gold ryng
    That home upbare.
The cordes that thei on ran
The Duk Betyse hom wan,   510
Mayd Medyore hom span
    Of mere-maydenes hare.

Ryght abought mydnyght
Seyd Syre Degrivaunt the knyght:
'When wolt thou, the worthely wyght,   515
    Lysten me tyll?
For love my hert wyl tobrest,
When wylt thou bryng me to rest?
Lady, wysse me the [beste],
    Gyf hyt be thi wyll.'   520
The burde answered [full yare]:
'Nevene thow that eny mare,
Thou schalt rew hyt ful sare,

518. me: MS e—damaged here
519. beste: MS damaged
521. full yare: MS damaged

---

503. *West-fal,* Westphalia, famous for its glassware from Carolingian times up to the sixteenth century. This kind of knowingness in fashionable description is curiously akin to that of contemporary writers of romance, like John Braine and Ian Fleming.

506–7. cf. *Sir Gawain and the Green Knight,* 854–7

510. *Duk Betyse* figures in the fourteenth-century *chanson de geste, Les Voeux du Paon,* though the allusion corresponds to no incident in that poem: the famous names are simply being used to heighten the atmosphere.

511. Betyse's lady was *Ydorus:* perhaps the poet has been influenced by the name of his own heroine, *Myldore.*

513ff. Note again the realistic treatment of the love-relationship: the lovers are not given the licence of French courtly romance.

And lyke hyt ful ylle.
Sertes, tho thou were a kyng,   525
Thou touchest non swych thing
Or thou wed me with a ryng,
      And maryage fulfylle.

Leff thou well withouten lette,
The ferste tyme Y the mette,   530
Myn hert on the was sette,
      And my love on the lyght.
I thought never to have non,
Lord nothur lemman,
Bot onely the allon—   535
      Cayser ne knyght,
Kyng ne non conquerour,
Ne no lord of honour,
And gyff hyt were the Emperour,
      Most proved of myght.   540
Forthy, syr, hald the stylle,
Whyle thou get my fadyr wylle.'
The knyght sentus thertylle,
      And trouthus thei plyght.

And whan here trouthus was plyght,   545
Than here hertus were lyght:
Was never faukons off flyght
      So fayn as thei ware.
Thai lay doun in the bede,
In ryche clothus was spred,   550
Wytte ye wel, or thei wer wed,
      Thei synnyd nat thare.
Than spekus the burd bryght

533. thought: MS thoughthe

---

534. 'husband, nor lover'
549–52. The practice of courtship in bed without final sexual intercourse by engaged couples survives as a folk-custom in a few societies today. It is probably wrong to regard it as a borrowing from folk-custom in the poem, however.

To Syre Degrivaunt the knyght:
'Swet syre, come ylke nyght,   555
    And loke how we fare.'
And the bold bachylere
Toke the damysele clere.
This [han] thei dured that yere,
    Thre quarterus, and mare.   560

(Degrevant repeats his visits, but is eventually spied upon by the Earl's forester, who tells his master. An ambush is prepared, but Degrevant and his squire defend themselves with great success. Eventually, in spite of the Earl's bluster, he is prevailed upon by his wife and daughter to make peace with the hero, and the marriage takes place. After a long and happy life, Myldore dies and Degrevant returns to the Holy Land, where he meets an honourable death.)

559. han: MS damaged
560. quarterus: MS . . . rterus

---

556. 'and let's see how we get on'
557–8. *i.e.* the two confidants—Degrevant's squire and Myldore's waiting-maid.

Bibliography

Texts

Editions of all the poems excerpted in this book are given in the notes to the texts. See also:

W. H. French and C. B. Hale, *Middle English Metrical Romances* (New York, 1930)

B. Dickins and R. M. Wilson, *Early Middle English Texts* (London, 1951)

K. Sisam, *Fourteenth Century Verse and Prose* (Oxford, 1921)

General Background

J. Huizinga, *The Waning of the Middle Ages* (London, 1924)

C. S. Lewis, *The Allegory of Love* (Oxford, 1936)

C. S. Lewis, *The Discarded Image* (Cambridge, 1964)

D. W. Robertson, *A Preface to Chaucer* (Princeton, 1963)

R. W. Southern, *The Making of the Middle Ages* (London, 1959)

Literary History and Criticism: Books

E. Auerbach, *Mimesis* tr. Willard Trask (New York, 1957). *See esp.* pp. 83–124

M. Bowra, *Heroic Poetry* (London, 1952)

D. Everett, *Essays on Middle English Literature* (Oxford, 1955). *See esp.* pp. 1–22

W. H. French, *Essays on 'King Horn'* (Ithaca, New York, 1940)

L. A. Hibbard, *Medieval Romances in England. A study of the Sources and Analogues of the non-Cyclic Metrical Romances* (New York, 1963), rev. ed.

G. Kane, *Middle English Literature* (London, 1951). *See esp.* pp. 1–103

W. P. Ker, *Epic and Romance* (New York, 1957)

W. P. Ker, *English Literature, Medieval* (London, 1912). *See esp.* pp. 102–43

Arnold Kettle, *An Introduction to the English Novel*, 2 vols. (London, 1962). *See* i. 28–42

M. Dominica Legge, *Anglo-Norman Literature and its Background* (Oxford, 1963)

R. S. Loomis, *The Development of Arthurian Romance* (London, 1963)

C. Muscatine, *Chaucer and the French Tradition* (Berkeley, 1960). *See* pp. 1–57

J. Speirs, *Medieval English Poetry: the non-Chaucerian Tradition* (London, 1957). *See esp.* pp. 99–262

R. M. Wilson, *Early Middle English Literature* (London, 1939). *See esp.* pp. 193–230

R. M. Wilson, *The Lost Literature of Medieval England* (London, 1952)

Essays and articles

R. Bromwich, 'A Note on the Breton Lays', *M.Æ.* xxvii (1957), 36–8

W. W. Comfort, 'The Essential Difference between a *chanson de geste* and a *roman d'aventure*', *P.M.L.A.* xix (1904), 64–74

Ruth Crosby, 'Oral Delivery in the Middle Ages', *Speculum* xi (1936), 88–110

N. E. Griffin, 'The Definition of Romance', *P.M.L.A.* xxxviii (1923), 50–70

D. M. Hill, 'Romance as Epic', *English Studies* xliv (1963), 95–107

J. R. Hulbert, 'A Hypothesis concerning the alliterative Revival', *M.P.* xxviii (1931), 405–22

J. Lawlor, 'The Pattern of Consolation in *The Book of the Duchess*', *Chaucer Criticism*, ed. Richard J. Schoeck and Jerome Taylor (Notre Dame, Indiana, 1961), ii 234–8. A criticism of attitudes on courtly love.

C. S. Lewis, 'The Anthropological Approach', *English and Medieval Studies presented to J. R. R. Tolkien*, ed. N. Davis and C. L. Wrenn (London, 1962), pp. 219–30

L. H. Loomis, 'Chaucer and the Breton Lays of the Auchinleck MS', *S.P.* xxxviii (1941), 14–33

L. H. Loomis, 'The Auchinleck MS and a possible London bookshop of 1330–40', *P.M.L.A.* lvii (1942), 595–627

L. H. Loomis, 'Chaucer and the Auchinleck MS', *Essays and Studies in honour of Carleton Brown*, ed. P. W. Long (New York, 1940), pp. 111–28

J. M. Manly, '*Sir Thopas*; a Satire', *Essays and Studies* xiii (1928), 52–73

G. Mathew, 'Ideals of Knighthood in late fourteenth-century England', *Studies in Medieval History presented to F. M. Powicke*, ed. R. W. Hunt, W. A. Pantin and C. W. Southern (Oxford, 1948), pp. 354–62

W. Oliver, '*King Horn* and Suddene', *P.M.L.A.* xlvi (1931), 102–14

G. V. Smithers, 'Story-Patterns in some Breton Lays', *M.Æ.* xxii (1953), 61–92

C. Strong, 'History and Relations of the Tail-Rhyme Strophe in Latin, French and English', *P.M.L.A.* xxii (1907), 371–417

A. McI. Trounce, 'The English Tail-Rhyme Romances', *M.Æ.* i (1932), 87–108, 168–82; ii (1933), 34–57, 189–98; iii (1934), 30–50

Glossary

abad *n.* delay, IX 129

abey *n.* IX 238, **at abey,** at bay, surrounded by dogs

abey IX 171 *see* **abye**

abye *infin.* pay for, buy dearly, VII 110, IX 171; *pa.t.sg.* **abugge,** I 219

ac *conj.* but, IV 42 &c.

admiral *n.* emir, III 154; **amerayle,** VIII 37

adrad *pp.* afraid, I 298; **adradde,** II 426

adreynt *pp.* drowned, IV 383

a-fine *adv.* to the end, IV 263

agesse *infin.* guess, reckon, intend, I 325

ay *n.* fear, IV 557

ays *n.* comfort, IV 225

aketoun *n.* acton, short tunic worn under the hauberk, VII 148

algate *adv.* at any rate, IV 217

alien *infin.* anoint, wash, V 10

almos-dede *n.pl.* acts of charity, IX 81

ambil *n.* amble, VII 173, **an ambil,** at a walking pace

amendement *n.* remedy, IV 186

amerayle *n. see* **admiral**

amorwe *adv.* on the next day, IV 167, 483

anker, *n.* anchorite, hermit, IX 63

anough *adv.* enough, IV 48

anuye *infin.* weary, irritate, II 374

apert *adj.* without disguise, IV 572

aplight *adv.* truly, V 149

arpthede *n.* people of long ago, IX 8

arewe *adv.* in a row, III 191

asay *infin.* test, try, IV 438, 554

asayleden *pa.t.pl.* assailed, II 501

aschape *infin.* escape, V 47

asowr *adj.* azure, VIII 41

aspie *infin.* spy, look out for, V 73

assembly *n.* joining of battle, VI 57

astate *n.* estate, (high) rank, VI 21

astirte *pa.t.sg.* leapt, II 143

astite *adv.* immediately, V 169

astrangled *pp.* choked, IV 382

aswon *adj.* in a swoon, IV 535

at-hold *infin.* restrain, IV 74

ato *adv.* apart, IV 111

atourned *pp.* equipped, accoutred, IV 277

atwo *adv.* in two, IX 330

aumal *n.* enamel, IV 350

auncetris *n.pl.* ancestors, men of former days, VI 5

aunters *n.pl.* chances, events, VI 5

auntrous *adj.* adventurous, bold, VII 197; **aunterous,** IX 377

aventours *n.pl.* happenings, events, exploits, IV 15, 21 &c.

avowed *pp.* coloured, adorned, IV 349

avyse *n.* opinion, IX 168

awedde *pp.* maddened, IV 386

ax *n.* axe, II 533

bachylere *n.* young knight, squire, IX 557

baiteth 3 *sg.pres.* baits, feeds, grazes, VII 201

bale *n.* trouble, ill, V 156

barbecan *n.* barbican, outer wall of a fortress, III 132

bare *n.* boar, IX 43

bare *adj.* bare, naked, deprived, V 142

barely *adv.* briefly, summarily, VI 68

barges *n.pl.* ships, VI 90

barre *n.* bar (of a door) II 433, 450 &c.

basnetus *n.pl.* basinets, light helmets, IX 306

bataild *pp.* embattled, crenellated, IV 346

batell *n.* battle array, IX 266, 273

bathed, *pa.t.pl.* bathed, IV 571

bede *n.* prayer, V 167

bede *infin.* present, offer, I 84

beyte *infin.* bait, II 479

bene *n.* petition, request, I 130

bent *n.* grass-slope, field, battlefield, VI 91, IX 277, 303; heath, pasture, IX 55, 200

bere *n.* outcry, IV 64

berien *n.pl.* berries, wild fruit, IV 244

berking *prp.* barking, IV 272

bermen *n.pl.* porters, II 120, &c.

besauntus *n.pl.* gold discs, bezants, IX 436, 491

bestadde *pp.* circumstanced, oppressed, VIII 130

bicolmede *pa.t.sg.* smeared, blackened, I 208

bicome *infin.* go, disappear; *pa.t.pl.* **bicome,** IV 274; *pp.* **bicome,** IV 180

bidde *infin.* instruct, command; *pa.t.pl.* **bad,** IV 74, 123 &c.

bidde *infin.* ask, ask leave, II 372

bydene *adv.* utterly, IX 175

bydyght *pp.* arrayed, IX 144

bihet *pa.t.sg.* promised, I 92

biis *n.* fine linen, IV 228

bileve *infin.* remain, be left, III 93; *pp.* **bileft** V 65

birthene *n.* burden II 59, 152

bite *infin.* bite, taste, drink, II 370

ble *n.* complexion, IV 441

blinne *infin.* cease, desist, V 54

blive *adv.* quickly, I 94, IV 128, 517 etc.

blosme *n.* blossom, IV 47

bloute *adj.* soft, pulpy, II 549

bodeth 3 *sg.pres.* heralds, foretells, VII 170

bokes *n.pl.* bucks, IX 43

boldyng *n.* encouragement, VI 14

bolle *n.* bowl, I 267

bondemen *n.pl.* husbandmen, peasant-farmers, II 266

bord *n.* table, II 361, IV 564

bordure *n.* heraldic border, IX 483

boru *n.* borough, town, II 25; **borw** II 99

bost *n.* pomp, display, IX 231

bote *n.* remedy, IV 538

bote *infin.* cure, make better, V 156

bountyveus *adj.* valiant, IX 311

bour *n.* bower, lady's apartment, VII 31

bourde *n.* enjoyment, IV 431; **bourdes** *pl.* IV 7, jests

bowe *infin.* go, take one's way, IX 55

brag *n.* ostentation, display, IX 231

brayd *pa.t.* drew (a sword), II 464

breche *n.* breeches, III 151

brembul-flour, *n.* flower of the bramble, VII 34

breme *adj.* bright, splendid, IV 47

brennen, *infin.* burn, II 166

brere *n.* briar, twig, IV 262

brevyt *pa.t.* set down in writing, VI 65; **brevyt** *pp.* VI 14

brid *n.* small bird, IV 291; **bryddes** *pl.* VIII 94

brigge *n.* bridge, II 125, 131

brymme *n.* (sea) shore, water's edge, VIII 142

brinie *n.* mail-coat, II 414

brisen *infin.* bruise, beat, II 474

bryttenes, 3 *sg.pres.* cuts to pieces, IX 306

broys *n.* broth, II 174

bronde *n.* torch, firebrand, VII 193

brondus *n.pl.* swords, brands, IX 476

brouke *infin.* enjoy, have, use, II 382

buernes *n.pl.* warriors, knights, men, VI 90

bughe *infin.* bow, writhe, twist, I 49, let fall

bulder-ston, *n.* boulder, II 429

bulmeth *3 sg.pres.* boils (?) III 198

bur *n.* I 8, 305 &c. *see* **bour**

burde *n.* lady, IX 521

burdon *n.* staff, I 205

buregh *n.* town, city, III 101, 106, 107, 125 &c.

burgays *n.* burgess, citizen, III 1; **burjays** *pl.* IV 490

burnes *n.pl.* IX 301, *see* **buernes**

burnist *pp.* burnished, IV 354

buskyd *pa.t.* got ready, betook himself, IX 130; **buskyd,** *pp.* adorned, IX 435

but *n.* throw, put, II 290

butras *n.* buttress, IV 347

butte *n.* a kind of flatfish, cf. halibut, II 11

carbunkulle *n.* carbuncle, VIII 55

cayser *n.* emperor, II 227, 364, IX 536

careful *adj.* full of care, unhappy, V 128

carl *n.* churl, slave, II 428

celure *n.* canopy, IX 482

cetewale *n.* zeodary, a plant of the ginger family, VII 49

charbugleston *n.* carbuncle, III 122

chartur *n.* contract, charter, IX 250

chaumber *n.* private apartment, IV 86, 182, 570; **chaumbur** IX 434

chaumpioun *n.* champion, athlete, II 257; **chaunpiouns** *pl.* II 265, 281 &c.

chaungyng *n.pl.* vicissitudes, VI 16

chas *n.* unenclosed hunting ground, IX 362

chawnses *n.pl.* chances, fortunes, VIII 132

chelde *infin.* grow cold, I 292

chere *n.* countenance, mood, manner, I 25, 207, V 96 &c.

cherl *n.* churl, thrall, servant, II 342

chese *imp.* choose, IV 203; **y-core,**

excellent, choice, noble, IV 91, 134; **ycorn,** *pp.* V 24; **icore,** *pp.* III 161

chevyt *pp.* achieved, brought about, VI 16

chinche *adj.* niggardly, mean, II 402

ciprees *n.* cypress, VII 169

cyprus *n.* cloth (?) of gold from Cyprus, IX 490

citte *pa.t.* cut, II 192

clanly *adv.* elegantly, VI 53

clapte *pa.t.* struck, II 453, 460

claré *n.* a drink of wine, honey and spices, II 367

clene *adj.* elegant, VI 77

clene *adv.* finely, IX 484

clepe *infin.* call, name, III 95; *pa.t.* **cleped,** IV 187; **cleped, y-cleped,** *pp.* IV 35, 38

clere *adj.* clear, transparent, IV 255, 344

cleven *infin.* cleave, split, II 167

y-clongen *pp.* shrivelled, IV 494

clowe-gylofre *n.* clove-gillyflower, clove (the herb), VII 50

coddys *n.pl.* pillows, IX 501

cofre *n.* coffer, chest, VII 53

colmie *adj.* sooty, dirty, I 226

comenci *pres.subj.* begin, IV 233

comessing *n.* beginning, IV 43

comyn *n.* cummin, a herb, VII 143

comoun *adj.* open, unenclosed common land, IX 143

compasyd *pp.* contrived, IX 484

conyngus *n.pl.* rabbits, IX 413

conseyl *n.* advice, IV 165

corage *n.* heart, spirit, mind, disposition, VII 68

cordewane *n.* Cordovan leather, VII 21

corelewe *n.pl.* curlews, IX 414

cormeraunt *n.* cormorant, IV 296

coround *pp.* crowned, IV 579

cost *n.* direction, quarter, IX 230; **costes** *pl.* coasts, regions, VI 83

costes *n.pl.* qualities, characteristics, behaviour, IX 364

cote *n.* cottage, IV 475

cote-armour *n.* surcoat, coat-of-arms, VII 154

couel *n.* cloak, garment, II 20, 110, 214 &c.

coupe *infin.* buy, pay dearly for, II 439

course *n.* VI 73 **by course,** in due order

cowthe *pa.t.* knew, was able, II 2, 23 &c.

crached *pa.t.* scratched, IV 66

crafte *n.* knowledge, VI 25

crapawtes *n.pl.* toadstones, VIII 22

creatours *n.pl.* creatures, IV 134

cres *n.* cress, as the type of something of little value, IX 191

crete *n.* wine from Crete, IX 416

cry *n.* cry, IX 77 an appeal for justice

crouders *n.pl.* fiddlers, players of the *crwth* IV 508

croun *n.* crown, IV 135, 221; crown of the head, II 152

culvart *adj.* false, faithless, III 135

cuntenaunce *n.* appearance, IV 279

curteys *adj.* courteous, well-bred, IV 28, VIII 2

custe *pa.t.* kissed, I 27

damisel *n.* girl, maiden, IV 76, 130, IX 385

darfe 3 *pl.pres.* need, have occasion, III 125

datheit *interj.* a curse on, II 176, 438, 526 &c.

deamondes *n.pl.* diamonds, VIII 58

debate *infin.* fight, contend, VII 156

declare *infin.* declare, set out in writing, VI 77

ded(e) *adj.* dead, IV 94, 386, 376 &c.

defens *n.pl.* fortifications, IV 34

degiselich *adj.* wonderful, IV 346

deynté *n.* delicacy, IV 240

del(e) *n.* share, part, II 70, 403; **dell,** IX 68

delen *infin.* share out, II 375; separate IV 111

demaynus *n.pl.* possessions, IX 69

denges 3 *sg.pres.* strikes, beats, IX 324

dent *n.* blow, stroke IX 340

dentethus *n.pl.* dainties, luxuries, IX 419

departed *pa.t.* divided, IX 330

der *adj.* bold, IX 25

dere *n.* dearth, II 76, 93

dere *n.* harm, injury, IX 344

dere *adj.* dear, II 91 &c.; **derrist** *superl.*, best, VI 39

dere *infin.* harm, injure, II 58

dereworthe *adj.* precious, IX 439

derffe *adj.* doughty, VI 84

desplaid *pp.* spread out, unfurled, IV 280

deviseth *pres.pl.* aim at, IV 298

dew *adj.* proper, VI 61 **was dew to,** belonged to

dextrer *n.* steed, war-horse, VII 201

diche *n.* moat, ditch, IV 347

dyght *pp.* adorned, VIII 16, 65; (IX 440 &c.) composed, IX 153,

dike *n.* II 562 *see* **diche**

dim *adj.* faint, IV 271

din(e) *n.* din, noise, II 499, 507

dint *n.* blow, stroke, II 446, 456; **dintes, dyntes** *pl.* VI 92; **duntes** *pl.* I 195

diol *n.* sorrow, lamentation, IV 184

divers *adj.* various, IV 350

donryght *adv.* utterly, completely, IX 140

dorte, I 10 *see* **darfe**

douhte *pa.t.* was of worth, availed, II 85

douhter *n.* daughter, II 329

drede *n.* dread, anxiety, II 80

drepen *infin.* kill, slay, II 422, 504; **drepit** *pp.* smitten, VI 9

drive *infin.* hasten, hurry, IV 127; *pa.t.* **drof**, II 432, 511

droghe *pa.t.* came, VI 88

dubbede *pa.t.* dubbed, conferred knighthood, I 121; **dubbed** *pp.* I 69

dubbing *n.* the act of conferring knighthood, I 60 &c.; adornment, decoration, I 186

dureth 3 *sg.pres.* extend, stretch, III 98

dured *pp.* endured, IX 559

dwelle *infin.* tarry, linger, remain, II 372

diune *pp.* wasted away, IV 247

eche *pron.* each one, IV 489

eft *adv.* again, IV 197

eie *n.* fear, terror, III 195

eighe *n.* eye, IV, 313, 577, V 76; **eighen** *pl.* IV 97

eyer *n.* air, VII 41

eyleth 3 *sg. pres.* ails, VII 73

eyr *n.* heir, II 345

eyre *n.* brood, IX 46

eke *adv.* also, IV 309 &c.

el *n.* eel, II 147

emerawdes *n.pl.* emeralds, VIII 80

endentyd *pp.* inlaid, IX 440

ennjoined *pa.t.* joined together, engaged, IX 273

ensoynd *pp.* excused, IX 275

er *conj.* before, IV 176, 242

erdyly *adj.* earthly, VIII 149

ere *n.* ear, IV 514

erl *n.* earl, II 250; *pl* **erls**, IV 188, 489

erndinge *n.* result of undertaking, I 203

ethelikeste *adj.superl.* most precious, III 167

euerrose *n.* rose-water, IX 399

euther *conj.* VI 57 **euther . . . . and . . . both . . . and . . .**

evyn *adv.* exactly, just indeed, VI 27

fader *n.* father, IV 29

fayne *adv.* gladly, III 82

fayned *pa.t.* falsified, VI 34

faire *adv.* naturally, V 204; properly, VI 82; **fayre**, fairly II 37

fairy *n.* faery, enchantment, IV 8, 269, 478, 548; **fairi**, IV 179, 390; **fayry** VIII 32, a magic contrivance

fairnise *n.* beauty, IV 42

fale *adj.* many V 150

fare *n.* state, V 33; behaviour, practices, VI 44

fare(n) *infin.* go, journey, fare, IV 590, VI 44; *pa.t.* **fore**

fast(e) *adv.* firmly, quickly, II 424, IV 80, 104

fastinde *prp.* fasting, II 117

faucoun *n.* falcon, IV 293, 298, 299

fawe *adv.* fain, gladly, III 91

fee *n.* property VIII 134, IX 88

feere *n.* III 76, **in feere**, in companionship

fey *n.* faith, IX 110, 120

feynit *pp.* invented, false, VI 18

feire *n.* fair, market, III 104

fel *adj.* cruel, deadly, fierce, terrible, VII 117; **felle**, VI 82

feld *n.* field, meadow, IV 46, VI 45

fele *adj.* many, II 30, IV 387, 508, VI 29 &c.

felun *adj.* savage, cruel, III 135

fen *n.* mud, II 123

fer *adv.* far, II 503; **fro ferne,** from afar; **fer** *adv.* further, VI 97

fere *n.* VI 18; **o fere**, in outward appearance

ferlies *n.pl.* marvels, VI 95

ferly *adv.* terribly, V 193

ferlik *n.* wonder, II 488

ferraunt *adj.* iron-grey IX 371

fers *adj.* fierce, proud, IV 279

festen *infin.* fasten, bind, II 424

fete *infin.* fetch, II 162, 354; *pa.t.* **fette**, VII 139; **y-fet** *pp.* IV 156

feteres *n.pl.* fetters, bonds, II 424

fyen *adj.* glad, happy, IX 146, 346

fille *n.* one's fill, IV 242

fine *adv.* very, IV 80

fir-sticke *n.* faggot, II 216

fiss(e) *infin.* fish, I 287

fissere *n.* fisherman, I 278

fit *n.* canto, passus, VII 176

fleye *infin.* fly, flee, II 452, 466; **fley** *pa.t.* IX 331

fleted *pa.t.* floated, drifted, VIII 98

flod *n.* sea, II 2

flours *n.pl.* flowers, IV 46, 146, 232 &c.

fo *n.* enemy, IV 98

fode *adj.* bold, V 192

foynede *pa.t.* lunged, IX 274

fole-hardi *adj.* foolhardy, IV 412

folwes *imper.pl.* follow, II 524

fonde *infin.* seek, try, V 210; IX 118, undertake, maintain, perform

fonge *infin.* get, take, II 15; III 193, receive.

forbar *pa.t.* spared, neglected, II 16

fordo *pp.* destroyed, III 201

foresteres *n.pl.* foresters, IX 114

foreward *n.* agreement, pledge, I 74

forleie *pp.* adulterous, III 194

forlived *pp.* mislived, tired of life, desperate, III 89

forloren *pp.* abandoned, forsaken, forlorn, II 22, V 126; **forlorn**, IV 113

forschreynt *pp.* shrivelled, IV 384

forthi *adv.* therefore, IV 447 &c.

forw *n.* furrow, II 344

foul *n.* bird, **foules** *n.pl.* IV 54, 261, 297

fouler *adj.comp.* sorrier, more miserable, IV 450

fowe *n.* variegated fur, IV 227

fowlehed *n.* foulness, V 212

fray *infin.* attack, raid, IX 237

frayne *infin.* inquire, VI 97

fraist *infin.* investigate, VI 97

free *adj.* noble, generous, free, VII 10, IX 33, 84 &c.

frek *adv.* quickly, eagerly, IX 373

frely *adv.* V 192 as *adj.* good, worthy

frese *infin.* freeze, IV 233

frete *pa.t.* gnawed, IV 525

fri *adj.* II 322 *see* **free**

frith *n.* woodland, IV 146, 232; **fryth**, IX 297

froted *pa.t.* rubbed, IV 65

frut *n.* fruit, IV 243

ful *adj.* full, IV 41, 46 &c.

ful *adj.* foul, II 215, 461, I 207

ful *adv.* very, IV 71, 177, 415 &c.

fundling *n.* foundling, I 42

gabbest 2 *sg.pres.* deceive, III 31

gabbing *n.* deceit, III 32

gablettus *n.pl.* small gables, IX 470

gaddes *n.pl.* goads, II 266

galantyne *n.* a sauce, IX 407

galun *n.* gallon, I 267

gambisoun *n.* cloth or leather tunic protecting soldier's trunk and thighs, IX 302

game(n) *n.* mirth, sport, II 355, IV 19, 301, IX 3; action IX 206; birds and beasts of the chase, IV 295, IX 56

gan *pa.t.*, *preterite auxiliary*, IV 63, 64, 104 &c, began; **gonne** *pret.pl.* IV 371; **gun** IV 490

gange(n) *infin.* go, walk, II 48, 97 &c; **gonge**, 2 *sg.pres.subj.* II 95

garysone *n.* treasure, III 2

garnettes *n.pl.* garnets, VIII 84

gart *pa.t.* made, caused to, IX 327, 338, 343 &c; **garte**, II 251

gate *n.* way, road, II 98, 139

geestours *n.pl.* story-tellers, VII 134

geete *n.* black marble, IX 469

geldene *adj.* made of gold, IX 280

genge *n.* company, household, retinue, II 38, 374

gent *adj.* well-born, well-bred, noble, III 41, VII 4

gentil *adj.* well-born, well-bred, charming, noble, IV 291, 449;

gest *n.* story, tale, V 159

geterne, gittern, *n.* a kind of guitar, with wire strings, IX 36

gyld *pp.* gilded, IX 397

gyle *n.* deceit, IV 9

ginne *n.* contrivance, scheme, tool; III 151 penis

girdel-stede *n.* waist, IV 252

gisely *adv.* skilfully, IV 285

givéled *pp.* heaped-up, II 66

gladlike *adv.* gladly, II 57, 399

gle *n.* minstrelsy, revelry, IV 253, 369, IX 34 &c; **glewe,** VIII 60

glede *n.* a live coal, II 121

gleive *n.* spear or lance, sword (?), II 387, 409; **gleves** *pl.* IX 279

glent *pa.t.* glanced, struck obliquely, IX 279

glides 3 *sg.pres.* II 490 flows

glysteryng *adj.* glittering, VIII 28

glotoun *n.* glutton, I 268

god(e) *n.* goods, property, possessions, sustenance, II 49, IV 216 &c.

gode *adj.* good, IV 244, 295, 331 &c.

godenisse *n.* goodness, virtue, IV 41

Goddot *interj.* God knows, II 48

gome *n.* man, VI 54, IX 302; **gume,** III 154

gonge II 95 *see* **gange**

goore *n.* the gore, or piece of a garment, also the whole garment, VII 77

grace *n.* (supernatural) grace, IV 533; **gras,** VII 119

graidly *adv.* readily, aptly, VI 54 carefully

grayn *n.* dye, VII 16 **in grayn,** of a fast colour

gre *n.* prize for victory, IX 96

gredest 2 *sg.pres.* cry out, IV 90

greythe *infin.* prepare, II 401

greyve *n.* an official in town administration, II 410; **greyves** *gen.* II 388

grene *n.* green, a grassy place, II 246, IV 58, IX 174, 235

grene *adj.* green, IV 339

gresse *n.* grass, IV 230; **grases** *pl.* IV 246

gret(e) *adj.* great, large, IV 226, 276, 573 &c.

grette *pa.t.* greeted, assailed, II 450

griis *n.* grey fur, IV 227

gripeth *imper.pl.* grip, seize, II 521; **grop** *pa.t.sg.* II 415, 529, 531; **gripen** *pa.t.pl.* II 429

grim, *adj.* awe-inspiring, IV 170

grom *n.* boy, II 42

gronge *n.* grange, farm-house, II 16

grot *n.* detail, IX 490

grounde *n.* ground, IV 545; **groundes** *pl.* causes, foundations, VI 80

growht *pa.t.* complained, lamented, VIII 117

gruf *adv.* face-down, VIII 104

grund-stalwurthe *adj.* very stalwart, II 277

habergeoun *n.* hauberk, mail shirt, VII 149

hayl *adj.* sound, wholesome, V 48

haynus *n.pl.* parks, IX 70

hayroun *n.* heron, IV 296

haithill *adj.* noble, VI 38

halke *n.* corner, I 231

halowed *pp.* honoured, IX 91

halowede *pa.t.* shouted, IX 236

hand-bare *adj.* empty-handed, II 18

happes *n.pl.* fortunes, VIII 99

hardi *adj.* bold, IV 27

hare *n.* hair, IX 512

hastelettus *n.pl.* pigs' entrails, IX 407

haukin, *n.* hawking, IV 294; **haukyng,** VII 26

haunt *n.* plenty IV 295

haunt *n.* abode, VII 99

hawberk *n.* mail shirt, IX 278, VII 151 (*see note*)

hed *n.* head, IV 135; **hade**, IV 377; **heved**, II 398; **hevedes** *pl.* VII 130

heighe *adj.* high, exalted, IV 26, 291, 312 &c.; **hey**, II 321, tall; **hexte** *superl.* II 330

heighing *n.* haste, IV 123

heldus 3 *pl.pres.* sink, IX 284

helm *n.* helmet, II 398

hend(e) *adj.* courteous, IV 549, VIII 12, I 261; prompt, ready, V 31

henged *pp.* hung, II 561

hepe *n.* hip (of the dog-rose), VII 36

herbarwe *n.* lodging, IV 470

here *n.* hair, IV 251, 492

y-heryghed *pp.* pillaged, IX 140

hernes *n.pl.* brains, II 447, 556

hert(e) *n.* heart, IV 324, II 448

hethe *n.* heath, IV 223, 229, IX 284

hethene *adj.* heathen, IX 119

hethenisse *n.* heathendom, foreign parts, IV 499; **hethennes**, VIII 37

heved *n.* II 398, *see* **hed**

hye *n.* haste, IX 221

hyght *pa.t.* was called, VIII 13

hilde *pa.t.* covered, V 118

hille *n.* hill, IV 340; **hyl**, II 142, a heap

hynthur *adj.* hind, hinder, VIII 102

hire *n.* hire, pay, II 158

hode *n.* hood, IV 215

hok *n.* hook, II 4, 352

hole *adj.* whole, sound, healthy, V 48

holtes *n.pl.* woods, IV 200

holwe *adj.* hollow, IV 254

hore *adj.* grey, IV 200

y-hote *pp.* called, IV 587, *see* **hyght**

hose(n) *n.pl.* hose, clothing for the leg, II 112 &c.

hovede *pa.t.* tarried, remained, IX 313

horse-knave *n.* horse-boy, groom, II 269

husbondus *n.pl.* manorial tenants, villeins, IX 139, 146; **husebonde**, husband, I 37

hwel *n.* whale (?) II 7

hwilgat *adv.* how, which way, II 88

hwit *adj.* white, II 368

icore, ycorn, *see* **chese**

ich *adj.* each, every, IV 144, 165, 240 &c.

ich *adj.* same, IV 49, 441, 526

ich *pron.* each one, IV 170, 281, 293 &c.

ichon *pron.* each one, IV 147

y-fere *adv.* together, IV 209; **yfere**, V 90

y-let, *see under* l

ilk *adj.* each, every, II 70 &c.

ilkan *pron.* each one, II 409 &c.

ilome *adv.* often, frequently, III 86

ymagerye *n.pl.* figures, images, VIII 96

ympe-tre *n.* grafted tree, orchard tree, IV 56, 152, 172 &c.

inow *adv.* enough, II 154, 161, 181 &c.

i-orne, *see under* o

i-quemeth, *see under* q

i-sterve, *see under* s

i-swoghe, *see under* s

yvele, ivele *adj.* evil, II 244

yvore *n.* ivory, IX 389

i-yolde, *see under* y

jacinctes *n.pl.* jacinths (precious stones), III 180

jambeux *n.* leg-armour, VII 163

jane *n.* a small coin of Genoa, VII 24

jepun *n.* padded tunic, IX 291

jesseraund *n.* coat of armour made of small rivetted metal plates, IX 291

joie *n.* joy, merriment, IV 6, 260, 577

jolif *adj.* gay, cheerful, IV 291

jolitee *n.* amusement, enjoyment, VII 131

joupe *n.* a loose jacket, II 406

karppe *infin.* speak, tell, IX 9

kaske *adj.* vigorous, active, II 480

kassydonys *n.* chalcedony (a precious stone), VIII 56

keling *n.* codfish, II 9

kempe *n.* champion, II 286

ken *infin.* make known, teach, VI 25

kende *adj.* kind, V 69

kepe *infin.* look after, attend to, IV 194, V 68; *pa.t.* **kepte**, II 129, watched, kept watch for.

kernel *n.* canal, conduit (?), III 119

kesten *infin.* cast, fling, II 423

kynde *adj.* inborn, naturally belonging to one, VI 70

kinneriche *n.* kingdom, II 226

kippe *infin.* seize, snatch, II 144

kirtel *n.* kirtle, short coat, IV 215

kythe *n.* one's own country, IX 298

kythe *infin.* show, make known, V 218; recognize, IX 364; *pp.* **kid**, II 310

kitte, *see* **citte**

knave *n.* boy, child, II 199 &c.

kne *n.* knee, IV 493; **knes** *pl.* II 541

kniht *n.* knight, II 396 &c.

knell *infin.* kneel, IX 327

knylle *infin.* ring, peal, IX 464

knokketh 3 *sg.pres.* knocks, IV 365

knoppus *n.pl.* knobs, ornamental buttons, IX 502

knoweleche *n.* recognition, IV 468

kok *n.* cook, II 124, 130, 141 &c.

koralle *n.* coral, VIII 82

korn *n.* corn, II 21

kowthe, *see* **cowthe**

krake *infin.* crack, break, II 164, 547

kradel-barnes *n.pl.* children in the cradle, II 551

lac *n.* blemish, IV 446

ladde *n.* serving-man, churl, II 406 &c.

lay *n.* lay, song, IV 585, 587, VII 57; **layes** *pl.* IV 3, 13, 20

layke *infin.* *see* **leyke**

lake *n.* fine linen, VII 146

lappes *n.pl.* folds (of a garment), VIII 102

lare *n.* learning, skill, IX 504

large *adj.* generous, IV 28

largelich *adv.* generously, fully, IV 437

late(n), 1 *sg.pres.* allow, permit, II 380; **lat** *imper.* II 411

latoun *n.* latten, an alloy of copper and zinc, VII 165

lauhwinde *prp.* laughing, II 196; **low** *pa.t.* II 153; *pa.t.pl.* **lowen**, II 306; **lough** *pa.t.* IV 300

laumprei *n.* lamprey, II 23; **laumpreys** *pl.* II 366

launcegay *n.* slender lance of hard wood, VII 40

launde *n.* glade, forest clearing, IX 239, 245, 290 &c.

lax *n.* salmon, II 6; **laxes** *pl.* II 146, 366

led *n.* cauldron, pot (orig. of lead), II 174

lede *n.* man, VI 62; **ledes** *pl.* IX 292

ledde *pa.t.*, II 37 **him ledde**, lived, managed his affairs; **ladde** *pa.t.* IV 570

leede *n.* people, VIII 150

leere *n.* flesh, VII 145

lees *n.* falsehood, VIII 38

lef *adj.* dear, IV 88, 392; **lever** *comp.* preferable, IV 163

ley *n.* lake, pool, IX 239

leyd *pa.t.* laid, IV 30

leyk *n.* game, sport, II 271

leyke(n), *infin.* play, take part in sports, II 200, 247; **layke**, II 261; *pa.t.pl.* **leykeden**, II 204

leme *n.* light, brightness, III 123

lemman *n.* dear one, beloved, III 21, VII 76, I 198 &c.; **lemon**, IX 62

lene *adj.* lean, thin, IV 445

lenge *n.* ling, a kind of fish, II 84

lenge *infin.* prolong, II 373

lep *pa.t.* ran, leapt, II 141, 416; *pa.t.pl.* **lopen**, II 535

leren *infin.* learn, II 49, 75

lernyng *n.* instruction, VI 32

lese *infin.* lose, IV 164; **y-lore** *pp.* IV 195, 531

lesing *n.* lie, falsehood, IV 451

lete *infin.* let, allow, lose, IV 163, leave, IV 265; **lete** *imper.sg.*, IV 100; *pa.t.* **lete**, IV 372, 60

letturs *n.pl.* writings, VI 26

leun *n.* lion, II 506

leves 3 *sg.pres.* believes, II 420

levedi *n.* lady, wife, IV, 39, 196, V 170 &c.; **levedis** *pl.* IV 75, 236, 284

lewtyng *n.* lute-playing, IX 38

lyard *adj.* spotted with white, or silver-grey, IX 76

lycorys *n.* liquorice, VII 49

ligge(n) *infin.* IV 60, II 54, 126 &c.; **lith** 3 *sg.pres.* IV 229; **liggeth** *pl.* IV 427; **liggeand** *prp.* IV 374; **lay** *pa.t.* IV 103, 119 &c.

light *infin.* shine, IV 357

lightnes *n.* gladness, VI 15

liht *n.* light, II 528

liif *n.* life, IV 88, 110, 163 &c.; **live**, IV 569; **lives** *gen.sg.* as *adv.* II 253 alive

liketh 3 *sg.pres.* pleases, IV 237, 435; **liked** *pa.t.* IV 515

limes *n.pl.* limbs, IV 157

lympit *pa.t.* stumbled, VI 36

lyng *n.* heather, IX 336

list 3 *sg.pres.* VI 20 **him list**, pleases him; **lust** *pa.t.*, I 28

lite *adv.* little, IV 244

lyth *infin.* listen, V 220

logede *pa.t.* lodged, dwelt, VI 62; **loggede**, IX 228, camped

loketh 3 *pl.pres.* IV 98; **loke** *imper.* IV 151; *pa.t.* **lokyt**, VI 36, made investigations

lording *n.* lord, noble, IV 26, 506 &c.

loth *adj.* hateful, V 22; unwilling, sorry, regretful, IX 195

lothli *adj.* loathsome, repulsive, IV 64; **lothlich**, IV 447

louerd *n.* lord, II 384, 420, 514 &c.

loupe *infin.* run, rush, II 440

love-drury *n.* passionate love, VII 183

love-longyng *n.* amorous desire, VII 60

lovesum *adj.* beautiful, amiable, IV 446

lowynge *prp.* glowing, IX 444

lusti *adj.* pleasant, VI 15

luthere *adj.* evil, bad, I 120

may *n.* maiden, V 108

may 3 *sg.pres.* can, is able to, IV 42, 102, 241 &c; **might** *pa.t.* IV 40; **mihte**, II 404; **mouhte**, II 470 &c.

maylus *n.pl.* coats of mail, IX 295

maister *n.* lord, master, IV 399

maystris *n.pl.* skills, feats of skill, IX 112

make *n.* match, mate, wife, VII 80

malais *n.* discomfort, IV 226

malvesyn *n.* malmsey wine, IX 423

maner *n.* kind, habit, custom, I 172, IV 417, 350 &c.

manhede *n.* human kindness, IX 83

mappemound *n.* map of the world, IX 31

y-marked *pp.* appointed, IV 534

maugre *adv. & prep.* in spite of, II 428

maulardes *n.pl.* mallards, IV 296

mawe *n.* maw, paunch, stomach, VII 111

mazelyn *n.* mazer, bowl of maplewood, VII 140

mecull, *see* **mikel**

mede *n.* reward, I 92

meene I *sg.pres.* mourn, III 69

meiné *n.* household, company, II 79, 86; **meney,** IX 134; **meyny,** VI 37

menske *n.* humaneness, courtesy, IX 83

menstraci *n.* minstrelsy, IV 288, 575 &c.

menstrellys *n.pl.* minstrels, VIII 60

merci *n.* mercy, IV 99, 498

meremaydenus *n.pl.* mermaids, IX 512

mervaile *n.* marvel, wonder, IV 395, 584

mese *n.* moss, IV 234

mese *n.* fault, misdeed, IX 190

messe-gere *n.* things used in the service of the Mass, II 328

mest *adv.* most, chiefly

mester(e) *n.* trade, business, I 171, II 75

mete *infin.* meet, IV 496

met *pa.t.* dreamed, V 25

mete *n.* meal, food, II 94, 104, IV 240 &c.

mevyt *pp.* moved, passed, VI 30

mikel *adj.* great, much, II 273 &c.; **miche** IV; **mecull,** VI 10

mynne *infin.* recall, remember, mention, VI 30

miri *adj.* merry, pleasant, IV 44, 48, 422 &c.

misdede *pa.t.* injured, offended, II 242, 243

misferde *pa.t.* II 508, **misferde with,** harmed, attacked

mislyken *infin.* to be displeased, I 47

missays *n.* discomfort, IV 248; **messais,** IV 311

mithe *infin.* conceal, II 198

mode *n.* manner, mind, V 98

moynelus *n.pl.* mullions, IX 467

moyste *adj.* new (of ale), VII 52

molde *n.* mould, design, IX 443

mon *n.* lamentation, IV 184

mone *n.* moon, II 528

mone *n.* II 68, **bi mine mone,** in my opinion

mone *n.* companion, I 150

mone *n.* companionship, participation, I 258

mot I *sg.pres.* must, IV 112; **most,** 2 *sg.pres.* IV 454; **mot** 3 *sg. & pl.,* IV 234, 111, 420; **most** *pa.t.* IV 219, 316

mowe *infin.* mow, II 491

nade *pa.t.* had not, IV 378

nail *n.* fingernail, IV 92; **nayl,** nail, spike, II 109

nakette *n.* precious stone; agate (?), mother-of-pearl (?), VIII 22

nam I *sg.pres.* am not, IV 416

nam *pa.t.* took, II 150, IV 140; **nome** *pl.* IV 78, 273, V 178 &c.; **y-nome** *pp.* IV 179, 551, 463 &c; **noome** *pp.* III 23, gone

narwe *adj.* narrow, IV 469

nas *pa.t.* was not, IV 84, 136, 340 &c.

nedes *adv.* of necessity, IV 454

neighe *adv.* nearly, IV 185

nempned *pa.t.* named, IV 586

nere *pa.t.* was not, IV 443; **nere** *pl.* IV 108; **nare,** IV 376

net *n.* fishing-net, II 4, 35

net *n.* ox, II 60, 276, 530; **netes** *gen.sg.* II 33

nevene *imper.* name, IX 522

neves *n.pl.* fists, II 556

newhen *infin.* come near, II 505

niht *n.* night, II 393 &c.

nil *pres.sg.* will not, IV 197, 318, 324

nis 3 *sg.pres.* is not, IV 117, 292, 538 &c.

nist *pa.t.* did not know, IV 274, 282, 480

nixte *adv.* nearest, beside, I 14
no *n.* a denial, IV 36
nobulle *n.* display, IX 92
noither *pron.* neither, IV 310
noither *conj.* neither, IV 332
nok *n.* corner, small part, II 72, IX 181
nold *pa.t.* would not, IV 126, 140, 266
none *n.* noon, IV 61, 358
none-tide *n.* midday, IV 483
nonskyns *adj.* of no kind, III 22
nome, *see* **nam**
note *n.* tune, song, melody, IV 588, IX 39; **notes** *pl.* notes, IV 424, 513, IX 426
notemuge *n.* nutmeg, VII 51
nouthe *adv.* now, IV 452

ofdrad *pp.* afraid, I 195
of-sende *infin.* send for, IV 414
ogee *n.* ogee, diagonal rib of a vault, IX 438
ogain *adv.* again, IV 127, 148
ogain *prep.* towards, IV 483
ok *adv. & conj.* also, II 129 &c.
ones *adv.* once, ever, IV 108; **onus**, VIII 112
one *adj.* alone, II 67, 186 &c.
onlepi *adj.* a single, II 344
onicle *n.* a precious stone, onyx (?), III 181
or *adv.* before, II 293
orchard-side *n.* the edge of an orchard, IV 52, 120
ordainy 1 *sg.pres.* ordain, IV 191; **ordeyned** *pp.* devised, IX 390
ore *n.* oar, II 525
i-orne *pp.* run, travelled, I 290
orrelegge *n.* clock, IX 461
ost *n.* army, body of men, IV 276, IX 229
other *conj.* or, IV 336
overkeveryd *pp.* covered over, IX 479

overraght *pa.t.* revised, VI 69
owher *adv.* anywhere, IV 17
owhen *adj.* own, IV 149, 257, 308 &c.
owth *pa.t.* ought, was obliged to, VIII 115

page *n.* page-boy, II 369
payndemayn *n.* fine white bread, VII 14; **paynemayn**, IX 401
pak *n.* company, gang, IX 334
pal *n.* rich cloth, IX 479; **palle**, IX 87
palfray *n.* palfrey, nag, IV 142
paniers *n.pl.* baskets, II 12, 57, 65 &c.
papejay *n.* popinjay, parrot, VII 55; **papegeyes** *pl.* IX 488
pappes *n.pl.* breasts, VIII 105, 111
parabolus *n.pl.* Proverbs, IX 447
parage *n.* high birth, III 149
paramoure *adv.* passionately, III 14
parfay *interj.* indeed, IV 301, 325, 368 &c.
parke *n.* park, enclosed land, IX 47; **parkes** *pl.* IX 70, 107, 143
parpon *n.* binding stone extending through a wall from one side to the other, 438
part 1 *sg.pres.* depart, leave, VI 96
pas *n.* pace, speed, IV 286
pavelouns *n.pl.* tents, IX 227
pelle *n.* skin (*i.e.* for the coverlet of a bed), I 23
pelle *infin.* go, hasten, II 62
pere *n.* pear (as a thing of no consequence), IX 348
perydotes *n.pl.* precious stones, greenish chrysolite, VIII 83
perreye *n.* jewellery, IX 487
pyght *pp.* set, VIII 17, IX 227
piler *n.* pillar, column, IV 353; **pyllorus** *pl.* IX 450
pyment *n.* a drink of wine, honey and spices, II 367
pine *n.* pain, suffering, I 162

pystolus *n.pl.* Epistles, IX 446

play *infin.* play, desport oneself, IV 52, VIII 137, IX 37 &c.; **pley(e)**, II 201, IX 51; **plawe**, II 200

playces *n.pl.* plaice, II 146

plain *adj.* smooth, even, IV 339

playnge *n.* amusement, VIII 6 sexual intercourse

playtede *pa.t.* dented, battered, IX 326

plas *n.* place of battle, IX 349, manor, estate, IX 138

pleye *infin. see* **play**

plenere *adj.* full, III 104

plist *imper.* plight, I 32

ploverys *n.pl.* plovers, IX 410

plows *n.pl.* measures of land, IX 69

poyned *pp.* embroidered, IX 499

poke *n.* bag, II 21

poudryd *pp.* seasoned, spiced, IX 410

pover *adj.* poor, IV 416, 472, 475 &c.

poverlich *adv.* in poverty, IV 222, 553

pray *n.* prey, IV 299

prest *n.* priest, II 468

priis *n.* value, VIII 19; **of priis**, precious, IV 37, 50, 235

priketh 3 *sg.pres.* spurs, rides, VII 42, 45; *pa.t.* **priked**, IV 127

prime *n.* prime, 6 a.m. or the period from 6 to 9, VII 113

prist *pp.* esteemed, VI 33

privé *adj.* secret, hidden, VII 89

proferi *infin.* offer, IV 420

prow *n.* advantage, IX 215

pruesse *n.* prowess, brave deed, I 178

purper *adj.* purple, IV 228

purtred *pp.* depicted, IX 457

putten *infin.* put, throw, II 294, 301; *pa.t.sg.* **putte**, II 302; **putten** *pl.* II 272, 281 &c.

qual *n.* whale, II 5

quath *pa.t.* said, IV 113, 162, 212 &c.; **quodh**, II 439; **quoth**, II 425 &c.

queynt *adj.* elegant, IV 285, 286

quen(e) *n.* queen, IV 37, 49, 57 &c.

iquemeth 3 *sg.pres.* pleases, I 107

quyrboilly *n.* boiled skin, leather, VII 163

quyschonus *n.pl.* cushions, IX 382

ram *n.* ram (the traditional prize in a wrestling-match), VII 30

rape *n.* haste, urgency, I 176

rappes *n.pl.* blows, VIII 108

raughte *pa.t.* reached, VII 20

real *adj.* royal, IV 342

reche 1 *sg.pres.* reck, care, IV 328; **recche** 3 *sg.pres.* III 90

red *n.* advice, plan, remedy, help, II 78, 472

rede *infin.* advise, IX 216

redi *adj.* ready, IV 366

redyn 1 *pl.pres.* read, IV 1

regni *infin.* reign, IV 411

renne *infin.* run, II 470, 543

renouns *n.pl.* renowns, fames, IV 188

reyde *pp.* drawn up, arrayed, IX 266

reyn *n.* Rhenish wine, IX 422

repeyr *infin.* resort, IX 47

reve *infin.* rob, III 134

revay *infin.* hunt or hawk along the banks of a river, IX 50; **reveyd** *pp.* driven, IV 68

rewe *infin.* regret, be sorry for, IV 556, IX 214; **me rews** 1 *sg.pres.* IX 366

rewel-boon *n.* ivory, from the teeth of whales, VII 166; **ruel-bon**, IX 437

reweli *adj.* sad, V 162

reweful *adj.* dismal, IV 100

rewethe *n.* ruth, pity, sorrow, V 92; **rewthe**, I 31

ribaudry *n.* ribaldry, lewdness, IV 7

ribbes *n.pl.* ribs, II 539

riche *adj.* rich, powerful, splendid, II 401, IV 67, 147 &c.

rydalus *n.pl.* curtains, IX 506

rig *n.* back, II 414; **rigge**, IV 486

right *pa.t.* corrected, VI 69

riht *n.* justice, due, II 349

riht(e) *adv.* direct, straight, II 24

rinde *n.* husks, rind, IV 246

rippe *n.* basket, II 143

ris *n.* twig, spray, IV 291

roche *n.* rock, cliff, IV 333, 335

rode *n.* complexion, face, IV 93, VII 16

rote *n.* root, IV 242, 246

rote *n.* musical instrument, lyre-shaped, IX 37

rounde *adv.* easily, gently, VII 174

rout *n.* company, suite, IV 269, IX 106

rowe *adj.* rough, unkempt, IV 251, 445

rowne *infin.* tell, VII 123

rowte *infin.* roar, II 550

safere *n.* sapphire, VIII 55

saler *n.* salt-cellar, IX 397

salve *n.* salve, healing ointment, II 474

same *adv.* together, IX 404

sanappus *n.pl.* tablecloths, IX 395

sardoines *n.pl.* precious stones, sardonyx, III 178

sautré *n.* psaltery, a musical instrument, IX 35

sawte *n.* assault, VI 57

schal 1 & 3 *sg.pres.* shall, IV 158, 193, 212 &c; **schalt** 2 *sg.pres.* IV 116, 153, 502; *pa.t.* **schuld**, IV 176, 356; **schold**, IV 453; **schust** *pa.t.* 2 *sg.* IV 556; *pa.t.subj.* **schuld**, IV 211

schar *pa.t.* cut, V 114

scharp *adj.* sharp, IV 525

schaved *pa.t.* shaved, IV 571

scheld *n.* 'shield', tough skin and flesh on the shoulders of a pig (see note) IX 406

scheltrom *n.* rank of armed men, IV 173

schenche *infin.* serve, dispense, I 250

schene *adj.* bright, fair, III 156; **shene**, VI 89, VIII 78; **schine**, IV 344

schent(t) *pp.* killed, destroyed, IX 94, laid waste, IX 138; **yschent**, IX 208

schert *n.* shirt, IV 216

schetus *n.pl.* sheets, IX 497

schewed *pp. see* **shewe**

schygynge *prp.* trotting, IX 345

schille *infin.* resound shrilly, IV 258

schille *adv.* shrilly, IV 90, 512

schine *pa.t.pl.* shone, IV 401; **schon**, *pa.t.sg.* IV 138

schyr *adj. see* **shir**

schkyll *n.* reason, IX 187

schore *n.* threat, menace, IX 152

schoten *pa.t.pl.* shot, assailed, II 503, rushed, II 477

schrede *pa.t.pl.* cut to pieces, IX 293

schrifte *n.* shrift, absolution, II 468

schulle *n.* plaice, II 11

sclavin *n.* pilgrim's mantle, IV 214; **sclavain**, IV 329

scochenus *n.pl.* escutcheons, IX 489

scrippe *n.* scrip, sack, I 205

se(n) *infin.* see, II 271, IV 197, 448; **seth** 1 *sg.pres.* IV 237; *pa.t.sg.* **sawe**, III 50; **say**, II 131; **segh**, I 232, 239; **seighe**, IV 133, 283; **sighe**, IV 341; **isighe**, I 301; *pa.t.pl.* **y-seighe**, IV 314

seche *infin.* visit, IV 418

sege *n.* warrior, man, IX 275

segge *infin.* say; **seyt** 3 *sg.pres.*; *pa.t.sg.* **seyd**, said; *pl.* **seyd, sayd**

segges *n.pl.* cuttle-fish (?), II 146

seyl *n.* sail, II 106

sele *n.* seal, II 7

selkouth *n.* wonder, marvel, II 309

selve *adj.* same, IV 327

sembling *n.* assembly, gathering, II 268

sem(e)ly *adj.* fair, pleasant, seemly, shapely, IV 397, VII 18, VIII 63

sendal *n.* thin silk, IX 501

sentus 3 *sg.pres.* assents, IX 543

serche *infin.* search, inquire of, VI 24

sere *adj.* various, IX 472

serjauns *n.pl.* serjeants, men-at-arms, III 143

sertes *adj.* certainly, VIII 32

servede *pa.t.pl.* deserved, II 553

sesyd *pp.* settled, IX 65

sethen *adv.* then, afterwards, IV 148, 573, 582 &c.; **sithen**, VI 66

sethen *conj.* since, IV 107, 455

sett *pa.t.sg.* set, IV 497; **sete** *pp.* seated, IV 506

shalke *n.* man, VI 72

shankes *n.pl.* legs, shanks, II 542

sheres *n.* shears, II 109

shewe *infin.* see, examine, II 492; *pp.* **schewed**, showed, IV 145

shides *n.pl.* kindling, pieces of wood split thin, II 167

shir *adj.* bright, II 166; **schyr**, IX 293

shof *pa.t.sg.* shoved, pushed, II 122

sholdres *n.pl.* shoulders, II 457; **shuldren**, I 232

shon *n.pl.* shoes, II 112

shonde *n.* shame, harm, VII 196

shope *pa.t.sg.* made, fashioned, VI 72; **shop**, II 351

shride *infin.* cloth, put on, wear, II 213

shuldren, *see* **sholdres**

sike *infin.* sigh, I 48; *pa.t.* **syght**, III 52, IX 209, 316

siker *adj.* sure, IV 27

sikerlich *adv.* surely, certainly, IV 557

sykyng *n.* sighing, VIII 124

syklatoun *n.* a costly cloth, VII 23

syle *infin.* fall, sink down, IX 343

simenels *n.pl.* kinds of bread or cake, II 31

symphonye *n.* some kind of musical instrument, perhaps a tabor, VII 103

sité *n.* city, VI 66

sithe *n.* time, occasion, II 30 &c.

sythe *n.* side, VIII 140

slak *n.* small valley, IX 333

sley *adj.* skilful, II 334

slen *infin. see* **slo(n)**

sleynte *pa.t.sg.* slunk away, withdrew, V 95

slenget, *pp.* slung, thrown, II 562

slydyn, *pp.* slipped, fallen, VI 6

slo, *n.* sloe, II 101

slo(n) *infin.* slay, kill, II 384, IV 318, V 22, 92; **slen** *infin.* V 9, 50; **sle** I *sg.pres.* VII 100; **sleye** 3 *pl.pres.* IX 432; *pp.* **slayn**, V 134; **yslayn**, IX 241; **slan**, V 188; **slaw**, IX 333; **slawe**, II 442, VII 114

slomeryng *n.* slumbering, sleep, VI 6

smale *adj.* slender, IV 95

smale *adv.* in small pieces, IV 524

smothe *adj.* smooth, IV 339

snewe *infin.* snow, IV 233

snute *n.* snout, face, I 226

so *n.* tub, pail, II 183

softe *adj.* gentle, mild, II 241

sojournd *pa.t.sg.* dwelt, IV 33

solas *n.* diversion, amusement, enjoyment, VI 22, VII 3

solas *infin.* entertain, IV 369

somyn *adv.* together, VI 66

sonde *n.* message, messenger, V 213

sone *adv.* soon, IV 57, 63 &c.

sonne *n.* sun, IV 138, 338, 358 &c.

soore *adj.* sorrel, reddish-brown, IX 76

sore *n.* trouble, sorrow, IV 249, 546

sori *adj.* wretched, miserable, IV 444

sothe *adj.* true, VI 11

souhte *pa.t.sg.* sought, II 335

soun *n.* sound, IV 258, 422

sounde *adj.* whole, safe, IV 578

sowdan *n.* sultan, VIII 86

sowel *n.* anything eaten as a relish with bread, II 19

sowne *n.* swoon, faint, III 48

sownyd *pa.t.* fainted, III 42

spac *adv.* quickly, at once, IV 329

spannewe *adj.* brand-new, II 218

sparcle *n.* a little spark, VII 193

spede *imper.* prosper, IX 212; *pa.t.* **spedde**, II 8

speke *n.* speech, report, II 196

speke *infin.* speak, IV 124, 208, 323; **speke** *imper.* IV 438; *pa.t.* **speke**, 310

spent *pp.* used up, finished, IV 201; **y-spent**, IV 185

sperus *n.pl.* spears, IX 319

spicerye *n.* a mixture of spices, VII 141

spyt *n.* rancour, IX 101

spray *n.* sprig, branch, VII 58

sprede *infin.* spread, grow, IV 53

spring *infin.* grow, burgeon, IV 53; *pa.t.pl.* **spryngen**, VII 48

squier *n.* squire, IV 72

stac, *n.* stack, pile, II 66

staf *n.* staff, II 529

staf-slynge *n.* sling attached to a staff or handle, VII 117

stage *n.* upper floor of a house, III 143

stalworth *adj.* stalwart, hardy, IV 27

stan-ded *adj.* stone-dead, II 454

star *n.* kind of sedge used for kindling, II 189

stareden *pa.t.pl.* stared, II 287 (*see note*)

stark *adj.* strong, stout, II 238

stede *n.* place, II 485, IV 193

stede *n.* steed, horse, IV 131, 147..

steked *pa.t.sg.* shut, fastened, V 122; **stoken** *pp.* VI 11

stere *imper.* control, govern, I 56

sterff *pa.t.pl.* died; **isterve** *pp.* I 311

stert *n.* moment, instant, II 512

stikest 2 *sg. pres.* stab; III 88; **styken** *pa.t.pl.* IX 281

stint *pa.t.sg.* ceased, refrained, V 109, IX 375; **stint** *pp.* IV 433

stirte *pa.t.sg.* leapt up, rushed, II 64, 124 &c.

stith *n.* anvil, II 516

stithe *adj.* stout, doughty, VI 7, IX 16

ston *n.* stone, IV 137, 183, 332, an anchorite's cell, IX 63

store *n.* livestock, cattle, IX 72, reserve supply, IX 148

store *adv.* greatly, strongly, III 116

stotede *pa.t.pl.* halted, IX 226

stounde *n.* time, IV 536, IX 29, 226 &c.

stour *n.* conflict, battle, VI 7, IX 281

straught, *see* **strecche**

strecche *infin.* go, IV 327; **straught** *pp.* VI 11

strete *n.* street, IV 495

strie *n.* hag, witch, II 248

striketh 3 *sg.pres.* glides, IV 238

stronde *n.* strand, shore, I 282

strong *adj.* strong, oppressive, II 93, shameful, II 54, rough, VIII 113

strout *n.* contention, strife, II 289

stroute *infin.* contend, make a disturbance, II 418

stuard *n.* steward, I 15 &c.

stub *n.* tree-trunk, IV 332

stuffed *pp.* thickly crowded, VIII 96

sturgiun *n.* sturgeon, II 5, 366

super *n.* supper, II 401

suet *pa.t.pl.* ensued, followed, VI 24

surkote *n.* surcoat, upper dress, VIII 100

swank, *see* **swinken**

swannes *n.pl.* swans, II 365

swatte *pa.t.sg.* sweated, VII 64

swerd *n.* sword, II 398, 441, IV 281 &c

swere *n.* neck, I 26, 208, 346 &c.

swete *adj.* sweet, IV 350, 400, 428 &c.

sweven *n.* dream, V 43

swiche *adj.* such, IV 303, 184 &c.

swilen *infin.* wash (dishes), II 169

swym *n.* dimness, oblivion, VI 12

swink *n.* labour, work, II 22

swinken *infin.* labour, work, II 50, 51; **swank** *pa.t.sg.* II 40

swithe *adv.* very, exceedingly, greatly, quickly

swoghning *n.* faint, swoon, I 66

swolowet *pp.* swallowed, VI 12

swoned *pa.t.sg.* swooned, fainted, IV 183; **iswoghe** *pp.* I 50

tabernacle *n.* canopied dais, IV 398

tabours *n.pl.* tabors, drums, IV 287

tabourers *n.pl.* drummers, IV 507

take *infin.* take; *imper.* **take**; **tok**, **toke** *pa.t.sg.*; **tok**, **token** *pa.t.pl.*

tane *infin.* take, VIII 138

te *infin.* go, approach, IV 198, 276, 304; **teth** 3 *pl.pres.* IV 260

teyte *adj.* active, eager, II 480

tempreth 3 *sg.pres.* tunes, IV 423; **tempred** *pa.t.sg.* IV 512

tenantrie *n.pl.* tenants' holdings, houses, IX 141

tene *n.* suffering, grief, VI 81, anger, IX 173

ter *adj.* difficult, IX 417

teres *n.pl.* tears, IV 313

testere *n.* canopy, IX 493; **testur**, IX 482

testimoyeth, 3 *sg.pres.* testifies, VIII 90

teth *n.pl.* teeth, IV 525

text *n.* text, words or account of an original authority, VI 51

tharnes 3 *sg.pres.* loses, is deprived of, II 552

thede *n.* district, country, IV 461, 480, 521

thee *infin.* thrive, prosper, VII 105

thei *conj.* although, IV 159, 233, 419

thenche *infin.* think, IV 359

therk *adj.* dark, IV 356

theves *n.pl.* slaves, serfs, II 419

thonge *pa.t.pl.* struck, beat, VIII 107

thonked *pa.t.sg.* thanked, IV 458

thornebake *n.* skate, ray, II 11

thorte *pa.t.sg.* needed, III 141

thral *n.* thrall, servant, I 46, II 347; **thralle**, I 41

thralhod *n.* thraldom, servitude, I 61

thrinne *adj.* three, II 13

thro *adj.* angry, IX 329

thrustelcok *n.* male thrush, throstle, VII 57

thurch *prep.* through, by means of, V 11; **thurth**, IV 223, 379, 522

thus-gates *adv.* in this way, II 37

tyde *n.* time, VIII 139

tide *v.* happen, befall; **tide wat bi-tide**, come what may, IV 325

tiding *n.* news, IV 83, 473

tired *pp.* clothed, adorned, IV 572

tobrest *infin.* break, burst asunder, IX 517

to-chine *pp.* scarred, IV 248

tome *n.* leisure, opportunity, VI 43

torfer *n.* hardship, VI 81

to-rett *pa.t.sg.* rent, tore to pieces, IV 67

to-rof *pa.t.sg.* smashed, broke to pieces, II 431

toun *n.* town, IV 222, 574; IX 142; **tun**, II 16, village

tour *n.* tower, IV 145, 231, 345, VII 194

touseled *pp.* tasselled (?) IX 500 (*see note*)

to-yede *pa.t.sg.* visited, went to, II 17

trayne *n.* stratagem, guile, VI 94

traist *infin.* trust, rely on, VI 17

tre *n.* tree, IV 254, 494, bar of wood II 272, 460, 521 &c, thwart, VIII 104

trechery *n.* treachery, IV 9

trewe *adj.* loyal, faithful, true, II 395, IV 340, 555 &c; **tru**, VI 17

trewelovus *n.pl.* fleurs-de-lis, IX 492

trewe-love-flour *n.* true-love-flour, Herb Paris, VIII 53

trye *adj.* excellent, choice, VII 144

triet *pp.* tried, proved true, VI 17

trifuls *n.pl.* nonsense, foolish lies, VI 43

trompour *n.* trumpeter, IV 507

trone *n.* throne, VIII 128

trowe *imper.* believe, IV 415

tru, *see* **trewe**

trumpe *n.* trumpet, IV 287

truse *n.* truce, VI 94

tumberel *n.* porpoise, II 9

tun, *see* **toun**

turbut *n.* turbot, II 6

turnet *pa.t.sg.* turned, perverted, VI 42

turven *infin.* strip, skin, II 168

turves *n.pl.* turf, peat, II 189

y-tvight *pp.* snatched, IV 178

umbistode *pa.t.pl.* stood around, beset, II 514

umbiyeden *pa.t.pl.* surrounded, II 481

unable *adj.* impossible, VI 46

uncouthe *adj.* unknown, IV 521

undernome *pp.* undertaken (a journey), gone, III 15, recognized, IV 306

undertide *n.* morning, noon, IV 62, 119, 167 &c; **undrentide**, IV 51

auderyete *pa.t.pl.* understood, realized, IV 562

unker *pron.gen.dual* of you two, II 521

unnethes *adv.* with difficulty, scarcely, III 20, IV 207, 402

unride *adj.* rough, clumsy, II 214, huge, II 434

unsemely *adj.* rude, VIII 108

unsound *adv.* grievously, IX 316

unspurne *infin.* kick open, I 218

upbare *pa.t.pl.* bore up, supported, IX 508

uten *adv.* out, exhausted, II 94

utmast *adj.* outermost, IV 343

vanyté *n.* illusion, VIII 33

veneyson *n.* venison, II 365

vernage *n.* sweet white Italian wine, IX 416

verrament *adv.* truly, indeed, V 80, VII 2

verrit *pp.* averred, VI 49

vile *adj.* miserable, IV 534

vyolet *adj.* violet-coloured, IX 382

visage *n.* face, IV 66; **vysage**, VIII 101

voided *pp.* departed, been banished, IV 560

vousour *n.* vaulting, IV 349

wale *infin.* to choose; **to wale** (to be chosen), conspicuous, excellent, VI 8

wayn *n.* wain, wagon, IX 147

wayten *infin.* watch, II 393

wan *adj.* pale, IV 94

warye *infin.* curse, VIII 115

warys 3 *sg.pres.* lays out, spends, VI 19

warld *n.* world, IV 389

warp *pa.t.sg.* threw, cast, II 311

wastel *n.* cake or loaf of fine flour, II 31

wawes *n.pl.* waves, VIII 106

wedde *n.* pledge, hostage, IX 318

weddewede *n.* widowhood, VIII 5

wede *n.* clothing, II 113, IV 132, VIII 147, armour, IX 220

weder *n.* weather, IV 255

wees, *see* **wegh**

wegh *n.* man, VI 19; **wees** *pl.* VI 23

weldus 3 *sg.pres.* wields, governs, IX 288; **weld** *pl.* IX 271; **wolde** *infin.* III 3

wemme *n.* spot, blemish, V 223

wene *n.* doubt, VIII 81

wene I *sg.pres.*, think, expect, assert, IX 17; **wenestu,** do you think?, II 426

wepe *n.* weeping, lamentation, IV 181, 220

wepe *infin.* weep, IV 104, 577

wepeing *n.* lamentation, IV 205, 208

wepen *n.* weapon, IX 271

wer *n.* war, VI 8

y-werd *pp.* worn, IV 227

werewed *pp.* mauled, strangled, II 554; **wirwed** II 560

werk *n.* work, occupation, IV 303, stone-work, IV 360

werne 3 *sg.pres.subj.* refuses, denies, II 176

wete *adj.* wet, IV 66

wexeth 3 *sg.pres.* grows, IV 48; *pa.t.sg.* **wax,** IX 193; **waxen** *pp.* II 43

wicke *adj.* wicked, wretched, II 215

wyght *n.* person, creature, VIII 149, bit, I 125

wyghtly *adv.* valiantly, IX 271

wiht *adj.* courageous, active, II 258, 314; **wyght,** IX 10, 150 &c.

wiif *n.* wife, IV 164, 322, 471 &c; **wif,** II 354; **wives,** *pl.* IV 385

wil *adj.* at a loss, bewildered, II 115

wille *n.* will, desire, IV 210, 247, 370 &c.

wille *infin.* desire, wish, intend (*see* **ichil, nil** &c.); **wiltow,** wilt thou; **wold, wald,** *pa.t.sg.*; **wold,** *pa.t.pl.*

win *n.* wine, II 368

winne *n.* pleasure, V 60

winter-schour *n.* winter-shower, IV 45

wyse *n.* manner, fashion, VI 65

wysshe *imper.* guide, direct, VI 4; **wysse** 3 *sg.pres.subj.* I 35

wyte *infin.* know, IV 2, VIII 81; **wite** 3 *pl.pres.*; **wist** *pa.t.sg.* IV

180, **wyste,** IX 115, **weste,** IX 286; *pa.t.pl.* **wist**

wite *infin.* rule, IV 192

witt *n.* wit, mind, IV 68; **wittes** *pl.*

witterlye *adv.* surely, V 77

wo *adj.* miserable, sorrowful, IX 299, 331

wode *n.* wood, IV 223, 258

wode *adj.* mad, II 416; IV 380, III 198

wodedowve *n.* wood-pigeon, VII 58

wodeleche *adv.* grievously, IX 320

wode-rys *n.* branch of a tree, *hence* wood, forest, IX 172

wolde *infin. see* **welde**

won *n.* quantity, number, II 274

y-won *adj.* accustomed, IV 303

wonder *adv.* very, extremely, IV 90, 342, 387

wone *n.* dwelling-place, IV 351; **woon,** VII 89

wonger *n.* pillow, VII 200

woon, *see* **wone**

wordyly *adv.* worthily, VIII 11

worms *n.pl.* serpents, IV 238

worshippe *n.* honour, dignity, III 10

worthe *pres.subj.* be, become, II 352; **worst,** 2 *sg.fut.* IV 156, 160; **worth** 3 *sg.pres.subj.* VIII 132

wosseyled *pp.* wassailed, drunk healths, II 376

wote I *sg.pres.* know, IX 38

wothes *n.pl.* IX 188; wanderings, ravages (?) *see note*

wounde *n.* wound, IV 379; **wundes** *n.pl.* wounds, II 484, 537

wowe *infin.* woo, I 168

wreche *n.* wretch, IV 530; **wroche,** IV 319

wreke *infin.* avenge, II 540

wryth *n.* anger, IX 299

wrythe *infin.* right, IX 368

writh 3 *sg.pres.* wrap, cover, IV 230; **wreighe** *pa.t.sg.* V 149

wrong *pa.t.sg.* twisted, contorted, I 206

wrote *infin.* grub, dig, IV 241

wroth, *adj.* angry, IV 108, IX 193

wund, *see* **wounde**

wurne *infin.* prevent, I 230

yarked *pp.* appointed, VIII 125; **y-yarked,** IV 533

yede *pa.t.sg.* went, II 26; **yeode,** I 3; **yoode,** IX 127

yeddyngus *n.pl.* songs, IX 429

yemede *pa.t.sg.* governed, ruled, II 225

yern *adv.* eagerly, IV 309; **yerne,** II 130

yeveth *imper.* give, II 161 &c.

yoode, *see* **yede**

yore *adv.* long ago, IV 545

yore, yare, *adv.* ready, VIII 125, IX 424